JEWISH ENCOUNTERS

---

Jonathan Rosen, General Editor

Jewish Encounters is a collaboration between Schocken and
Nextbook, a project devoted to the promotion of Jewish literature, culture, and ideas.

# JEWISH ENCOUNTERS

*Maimonides*

# SHERWIN B. NULAND

# MAIMONIDES

NEXTBOOK · SCHOCKEN · NEW YORK

Schocken and colophon are registered trademarks of
Random House, Inc.

Library of Congress Cataloging-in-Publication Data
Nuland, Sherwin B.
Maimonides / Sherwin B. Nuland.
p.   cm.—(Jewish encounters)
Includes bibliographical references.
ISBN 0-8052-4200-7
1. Maimonides, Moses, 1135–1204.   2. Rabbis—Egypt—
Biography.   3. Jewish scholars—Egypt—Biography.
4. Jewish philosophers—Egypt—Biography.   5. Jewish
physicians—Egypt—Biography.   I. Title.   II. Series.
BM755.M6N85 2005      296.1'81—dc22
2005041651

www.schocken.com
Printed in the United States of America
First Edition
2   4   6   8   9   7   5   3   1

# CONTENTS

# PROLOGUE

The waters compassed me about, even to the soul:
the depth closed me around about, the weeds were
wrapped about my head.

JONAH 2:5

So cried out Jonah to the Lord, recalling how he had been "cast into the deep, in the midst of the seas," before being taken up into the capacious warm body of the great fish. He had done what he could, to avoid the impossible task for which he was chosen by a power whose determination was not to be escaped.

And so, too, I cried out to Jonathan Rosen, the general editor of this new series of books on Jewish themes, when I had for several months been immersed in the deep, inky waters of the vast Maimonidean literature, and not yet sighted a whale. I was being suffocated by weeds so densely wrapped about my head that, emulating Jonah, "I cried out by reason of my affliction" and begged to be relieved of a burden for which I had become certain that I was incompetent.

But Jonathan would hear none of it; I was not to be

allowed the flight to Tarshish and the release for which I so desperately yearned. Though I bombarded him with the names of scholars who had spent distinguished careers swimming comfortably in the Judaic and Aristotelean seas in which I was being drowned, Jonathan rejected them all. There had been several reasons that I—rather than an acknowledged authority—had been chosen for this mission, he replied to my importunings. He did not want a scholar steeped in the complexities of his subject's philosophy; he wanted a writer, who might seek out the essence of the man and tell the story of his lifelong journey toward understanding. Mainly what he was seeking, he explained, was an encounter between a contemporary observer and that towering figure from the Jewish past. Is there some common ground on which Rabbi Moses ben Maimon—commonly called by the acronym "the Rambam" but since the Renaissance more often known by the Hellenized appellation—can walk together with a man or woman of today? Are the issues that absorbed him so different from those with which we grapple in our secular era, that his memory can only be iconic rather than meaningful? In the more restricted sense, how does a Jewish doctor of the twenty-first century relate his sense of calling to the legendary Jewish doctor of the twelfth? Is it, in fact, even possible that anyone other than the small cadre of dedicated and deeply learned Maimonidean scholars can discover any sort of intellectual or emotional relationship with that great man of so long ago? Can we in our time recognize in him attributes we see in ourselves, or is he so removed from the experience of a present-day mind that we can only study him, but never fully comprehend who he was? "If Maimonides is lost to you," wrote Jonathan, "then he is lost to all of us."

And with those words, I decided to become Everyman. Not yet a bit less fearful of submitting a simplistic, superficial, or error-filled manuscript, I returned—resigned, though still reluctant—to the confrontation with my ignorance. I began reading again, immersing myself once more in the very waters from which I had sought rescue. And like many another drowning man, I one day unexpectedly found a buoyant object to which I might cling, at first desperately and then gradually with an increasing sense that I might yet be saved, and my literary undertaking with me. It came in the form of a single sentence written by one of the scholars whom I had recommended to Jonathan Rosen. In his introduction to Jacob S. Minkin's 1987 volume *The Teachings of Maimonides*, the eminent historian Rabbi Arthur Hertzberg had written, "Distinguishing between what we learn from Maimonides as he would have wanted us to learn from him, and what we make of him because that is what we want to hear, remains an insoluble problem."

I had already begun to perceive through the mists of my vague comprehension that many of the twentieth-century commentators on the Rambam had made interpretations that reflected their own religious or historical worldviews; that hyperbole and hagiography were common; and that an element of the muddling factor that historians call presentism—seeing the events of the past through the prism of today's values and knowledge—existed in far too many of the books and essays of even the most authoritative biographers. In each generation, scholars have found in Maimonides what they have wished, or needed, to find.

And of course, this last observation describes a state of affairs that is not all to the bad. Much the same might be said of the Bible, of scripture in general, of historical events and trends, and it is certainly true of the Constitution of the United States or that of any other democracy. Particularly in biography, constant reinterpretation can be a source of strength in a body of writing or knowledge, if one can but avoid the presentism and the exaggerating distortions that too often accompany it. As for the subjectivism, that is not in itself necessarily an obstacle, because a degree of subjectivity can only benefit the freshness of commentary. And freshness of commentary is, after all, the hallmark of the Rambam's contribution to religious thought. All of this was very reassuring to me as I thought over my communications with Jonathan Rosen.

Armed with these new realizations, I returned to the work; the present volume is its issue. This book is, quite simply, the outcome of the ancient Jewish dictum that one is not permitted to turn away from a responsibility, though it may prove impossible to bring it to a state of finality. And that, too—the impossibility of ultimate completion—is a good thing for this enterprise, because there will never be a finality in the interpretation of the Rambam's body of work or of understanding the events of his life, nor should such a thing be sought. Setting aside a bit of remaining trepidation, I continued to read and to study and to ruminate and to discuss with any colleague I thought knowledgeable (and some, chosen quite deliberately for this reason, who were not). In time, the turbulent seas somehow began to calm themselves, although at first ever so slowly. After some months, I really came to believe that I could see just a bit into the mind of the man I had been taught since childhood to revere, though so much of him had been unknown or at least obscure to me. With further study came further understanding. Of course, the mind I was seeing into was as much my own as his.

What is presented in these pages is, as Maimonides himself might have put it, a guide for the perplexed—those many like me who have known of Maimonides all of our lives and familiarized ourselves with just enough of him to believe, whether justified or not, that we have some modicum of understanding, but that it is never quite enough. To the majority of us, he has been little more than an honored name. And yet, some of us have frequently recited his Thirteen Principles of the Faith in our synagogues; some of us have had our photographs taken alongside his bronze statue in the Plaza of Tiberiades in Cordoba; some of us have made the pilgrimage to the site believed to be his grave in Tiberias; some of us have attended lectures about him by learned authorities; some of us have tried to learn more by occasionally spending an evening reading directly from *The Guide for the Perplexed*, and found much of its text well-nigh impossible to comprehend; some of us have pored over the large volume of twentieth-century literature about his teachings; some of us have even ventured into the pages of his *Mishneh Torah* to clarify a point of Jewish law, without so much as wondering about the man behind the words; some of us have donated funds to support a Maimonides school or hospital; and some of the doctors among us have belonged to a professional group in our communities called the Maimonides Medical Society.

I have done almost all of these things, and yet remained perplexed, needing a guide. The attempt to learn that was involved in producing this volume has been that guide. I have written it in much the same way as Maimonides wrote his *Mishneh Torah*, a book brought forth to elucidate Jewish law, or halakha, to the Everyman who would read it. It is not a book for scholars. Its aims, like the Rambam's, are clarity and conciseness; its purpose is to make Maimonides accessible to myself and therefore to others. To understand this little volume of mine, no previous knowledge of Moses ben Maimon or of his era is required, nor of philosophy, medicine, Judaica or academic methods. It is accordingly without references that might distract the general reader; it is completely the product of the understanding to which I have come after a long voyage of study; in emphasis and interpretation, it is without any attempt to avoid a certain level of personal viewpoint and subjectivity; on reaching its last page, each reader must decide individually whether he or she is any closer to answering the questions posed in the third paragraph of these introductory thoughts. I offer my book as this Jewish doctor's study of the most extraordinary of Jewish doctors.

*Maimonides*

# My Son, the Doctor:
# Jews and Medicine

Why is it, in fact, that so many Jews have become doctors? It is fitting to consider that question before embarking on a study of the life and thought of a man who personified the grand tradition, and whose teachings contributed so much to it. Here follows a twice-told tale that bears telling once again:

Imprisoned in a tower in Madrid, disabled by syphilis and further weakened by an abscess in his scalp, the French king Francis I asked of his captor, the Holy Roman Emperor Charles V, that he send his finest Jewish physician to attempt a cure. At some point soon after the doctor arrived, Francis, in an attempt at light conversation, asked him if he was not yet tired of waiting for the Messiah to come. To his chagrin, he was told that his healer was not actually Jewish but a converso who had long been a baptized Christian. Irate, Francis dismissed him and arranged to be treated by a genuine Jew, brought all the way from Constantinople.

Apocryphal or not, this charming little story has endured because it illustrates the position of the Jewish doctor during the Middle Ages and Renaissance. The narrative's supposed events took place at a fixed point in time, some years before the death of Francis in 1547, but they form part of a genre of anecdote that had existed for centuries. Though not as pervasive as it once was, the legend of the Jewish doctor's special skills is still current today, enduring in attenuated form alongside the legend of the profession's attractiveness to young Jews as a career. Intertwined with myth, the legendary relationship between the Jew and the art of healing continues to evoke a variety of responses, ranging from humorous comment to scholarly study.

To explore that relationship, several questions are easily framed and may be succinctly stated: Why have so many Jews been drawn to the study of medicine, far out of proportion to their numbers? Why have so many achieved distinction, far out of proportion to their numbers? And why, at least in centuries past, have Jewish doctors been thought to have accomplished so many more cures than their gentile counterparts, far out of proportion to their numbers?

Not surprisingly, the answers to these questions are multifactorial, multilayered, and multigenerational. But like so many multiplicities, they can be comprehended by recognizing that the answers are ultimately woven into a unity, not only of origin but of intent. Though the origin and the intent are now obscured by strata of time and cultural change, they are nevertheless there to see, if we are willing to look closely and cast aside—even if briefly—the religious skepticism of our age.

As in so many areas of Jewish questing, we can serve our purpose no better than by turning to the writings of Maimonides, in this case the fifth of the so-called Eight Chapters, or *Shemonah Perakim*, with which he prefaced the *Pirkei Avot (Ethics of the Fathers)* sections in his *Commentary on the Mishnah*, completed in 1168 when he was thirty years old. He there articulates a theme that would continue to appear in his writings for the rest of his life, summarized by his saying that the real purpose of wealth or any other acquisition

> should be to expend it for noble purposes, and to employ it for the maintenance of the body and the preservation of life, so that its owner may obtain a knowledge of God, in so far as that is vouchsafed unto man.
>
> From this point of view, the study of medicine has a very great influence on the acquisition of the virtues and of the knowledge of God, as well as on the attainment of true spiritual happiness. Therefore, its study and acquisition are pre-eminently important religious activities.

It was a Maimonidean precept that the purpose of keeping the body healthy is to enable the unhindered pursuit of knowledge of God, and of the perfect morality for which God is the model; the study of medicine is a religious activity. In saying this, Maimonides was echoing a thesis promulgated by the rabbis of the Talmud, who spoke of the physician as a messenger—or in certain ways even a partner—of God, and essential to the pursuit of an understanding of God's ways.

Though this is a Talmudic concept, it has its origins and inspiration—as do all the rabbinic writings—in the Torah. The stringent directives about public health, hygiene, preventive medicine, and sanitation laid out in Leviticus are expanded in the Talmud to cover every facet of personal behavior. The aim of these injunctions being cleanliness in the presence of God, the underlying message of the Talmudic sages is the biblical link between physical and moral purity, always emphasizing that maintenance of health is maintenance of life, the obligation of every Jew, though it might mean disobeying commandments. All Jewish law, even the Decalogue, may be violated in the interest of saving a life, the only exceptions being the injunctions against blasphemy, adultery, incest, and murder. "First choose life," enjoins God, linking the acceptance of God's precepts to the embrace of life. And by the very word *choose*, God makes it clear that man has free will.

It is in the notion of free will, I believe, that the essence of the Jewish approach to healing is to be found. The concept is repeatedly proclaimed in scripture, in the rabbinic literature, and in the writings of Maimonides. In these latter, it sometimes appears in lengthy expository passages and sometimes simply stated, as in the fifth chapter of Book I of the

*Mishneh Torah:* "Free will is bestowed on every human being." The Rambam had already written in the last of the Eight Chapters, "Our Torah agrees with Greek philosophy, which substantiates with convincing proofs that a man's actions are in his own hands; no compulsion is exerted and he is constrained by nothing that is external to himself."

Throughout the sacred writings, one is aware of the tension between the concept of God's will and the concept of human free will, manifest in an unspoken compromise that leaves care of the body to man—the intervention of God is not to be assumed. In this, the rabbis of the Talmud are rather like the Greeks, whose most lasting contribution to medical theory was to separate their worship of the gods from their nature-based methods of diagnosis and therapy. This approach is exemplified by the Hippocratic Oath and the entire corpus of classical Greek medical literature, in which the physicians swear by Apollo and Aesculapius, and then go on to proclaim the principles of a school of healing independent of any direct reliance on these or any other gods. Not only that, but some of the leading practitioners of Hippocratic medicine saw the study of their art as a way of understanding the divine, just as the Jews did. And they went even further. Galen of Pergamon, the most influential physician who has ever lived, believed that the proper way to worship the Divinity is not with prayer and sacrifice but with experiment and observation. Late in the second century C.E. , he described his greatest anatomical work, *De Usu*

*Partium*, as "the sacred discourse which I am composing as a true hymn of praise to our Creator." To him, learning about the body was the sure way to learn about the godhead. He wrote:

> And I consider that I am really showing him reverence, not when I offer him unnumbered hecatombs of bulls and burn incense of cassia worth ten thousand talents, but when I myself first learn to know his wisdom, power and goodness and then make them known to others.

Galen's way of knowing and making known was to experiment on animals in order to learn and then demonstrate the principles of anatomy and physiology. Though he believed that the divinity he called the Creator made the universe and everything in it according to a preordained plan, he never called on anything but his own skill in treating the sick. From the beginning, this was precisely the way in which Jewish doctors have approached the healing of their patients. In fact, their entire system of medicine was Greek during the days of Maimonides and for centuries afterward. There was never a Jewish medicine in the same way that there was an Egyptian or a Chinese or an Ayurvedic or a Western medicine. In the Middle Ages as today, Jewish medicine has been the medicine of the culture in which it is practiced. In Talmudic times, it was strongly influenced by the heritage of the Greeks, and not only because of their similar notions concerning the physician's independent role in healing.

The remarkably knowledgeable concepts of anatomy and physiology—as well as preventive and clinical medicine—found in the Mishnah and Gemara can be traced to a broad familiarity with Hippocratic and Galenic understanding of such matters, and the influence of Hellenism.

If its function is to help man know God and to achieve the moral life, then healing must be based on ethical principles. Here, too, the Greek and the Jewish systems of medicine were parallel. Just as they are credited with being the first to separate religious faith from the treatment of disease, so also have the Greeks been credited with introducing ethics into the teachings of medical care. But the Torah, of course, preceded them. Either way, the interlocking methods and aims of the Jewish and the Greek physicians—based partly on shared notions of the Divinity's distanced role and partly on the commingling of cultures during the Hellenistic period of about 280 to 160 B.C.E.—would have vast implications in creating the background against which the three questions have been framed, which are here being addressed.

Even the origin of the Hebrew word for doctor, *rofe*, has within it the implication of independent action on the part of the physician. It means "to heal" in the sense of repairing. The basic image is the mending of a torn place, or the sewing of a seam to bring parts together. As "raphe," the word exists in modern anatomic terminology, to designate any of several places in the body where tissues from each side are joined in the midline. It appears—in the word *rafa*—as healing by God in Numbers 12:13 and Jeremiah 3:22

and 30:17, among other places. Applied to healing by humans, it is a reference that requires the hands of the practitioner and the actual doing of something; it is interpreted as a human intervention. Modern dictionaries erroneously trace the etymology of "raphe" to Greek, attesting once again to the mutual Hellenistic influence of one culture upon the other.

And so, the rabbis of the Talmud taught in the presence of a heritage of ethics and with the conviction that the preservation of life is a basic teaching of their religious system of values, to be carried out by human action and existing as an instrument of Divine will, and yet being applied independently of the Divinity's direct intervention. Though God is the ultimate healer—and indeed, in several dramatic biblical passages God chooses to intercede in order to either cause or cure illness—God is not to be used by mankind as a medicine. When sickness occurs, a doctor is to be sought out, a dictum clearly articulated by Maimonides in *Pessahim* IV of his *Commentary on the Mishnah:* "One who is ill has not only the right but also the duty to seek medical aid."

But the Jewish doctors of the time entered into their work with yet another assumption, which may be of critical importance in their history of accomplishment. This was the concept—articulated centuries later in the Shulhan Arukh—that the *rofe*, though acting independently and with free will, is the individual messenger or deputy of God; he is therefore irreplaceable in healing by anyone else. This specificity was interpreted to mean that he himself must respond when called upon, because it may be in the Divine will that he alone is capable of that particular mission of healing. To this tradition may be traced the sense of personal responsibility—or, as today's bioethicists might put it, the deontologic obligation—that has characterized those physicians determined to excel because they are committed to the duty imposed by their own uniqueness. Such values as these are not easily thrown off with the passage even of centuries, because they are transmitted from teachers to pupils in a tradition going back millennia. Though they are hardly any longer uniquely Jewish, they entered the medical culture with monotheism.

It is in the time of the Talmudic sages—the third to the sixth centuries C.E.—that the relationship between Jews and medicine began to form the social foundation by which it would be characterized to the present day. The rabbis were not bloodless scholars, but committed members of the community whose experiences of daily life equipped them to understand the moment-to-moment existence they addressed in their discussions of the Law. They lived in the real world, in which prayer and cogitation were considered insufficient without real engagement and real work. Their position would much later be stated by Nahmanides of Aragon, a rabbi of the thirteenth century who wrote, "It is part of the service of the Lord to attend to the affairs of the world." It is hardly a source of wonder that 213 of the 613 commandments enumerated by the sages and eventually codified by Maimonides have in one way or another to do with care of the body.

Being committed to a principle that the Talmudic sage Rabbi Zadok articulated with the words (later reiterated by Maimonides), "Make not of the Torah a crown wherewith to aggrandize thyself, nor a spade wherewith to dig" (and also stated by the great Hillel, who said, "Whosoever derives a profit for himself from the words of the Torah is helping in his own destruction"), the scholars of that period and afterward rejected payment for their religious services and sought secular employment. Given the Jewish emphasis on bodily health, it was only natural that some of them turned to healing as a source of income. It was in this way that the association of medical skills and rabbinic wisdom became, in a sense, formalized. From that point on and continuing well into the Renaissance, many physicians were rabbis. It has been estimated that during the Arabic period, approximately half of the Jewish doctors were rabbis. It should not be forgotten that the word *rabbi* derives from the Hebrew *rav*, meaning "teacher"; "doctor" derives from the Latin verb *docere*, meaning "to teach."

Unlike the medical practitioners of medieval Christian Europe, the majority of whom were self-proclaimed and sometimes illiterate healers, the Jewish physician was likely to have mastered the intricacies of his art as taught by skilled members of the profession. This meant not only that so many of them were valued because they were among the most secularly educated of the Jews, but also that they were leaders of the communities in which they lived. The tradition that doctors were among the leadership enhanced the prestige and social standing of the profession, and as Jewish doctors became more sought out by prominent Muslims and Christians, they gradually came to represent their coreligionists before the gentile rulers. Power often passed into their hands, and increasingly many of them were looked to as men of authority not only among the Jews but in the dominant non-Jewish world as well. In these ways, the stature of the Jewish physician became ever more elevated even during centuries of unrelieved oppression. This would be vastly enhanced following the Enlightenment of the eighteenth century, when the lowering of cultural barriers allowed even greater social mobility and contact between Jews and Christians. During those times, when the education of Jews was gradually becoming less confined to religious schooling, the esteem in which secularly knowledgeable doctors were held became even greater. Comfortable in both worlds, they were seen as idealized figures who attained worldly accomplishment while resisting assimilation.

The gentile seeking out of Jewish physicians had several causes, the first of which is simply that any individual among them was, for the reasons given, more likely to be skilled than his non-Jewish counterpart, especially in Christian lands. Some achieved considerable renown, and their services were requested by powerful people separated by long distances, adding to the general impression among the multitude of citizens that there was something special about

Jewish healers. Such an impression was hardly lessened by a disquieting perception that these devious strangers in their Christian midst, who spoke among themselves in an inscrutable tongue and called upon a God whose ways seemed so cryptic, had special hidden knowledge, perhaps of the occult. And thus, their very differentness and the apprehension it aroused meant that superior, even if possibly demonic, healing gifts were often attributed to them not only by commoners but by the nobility as well. Likely, the mystique of the Jewish doctor not only added to his reputation, but had a placebo effect on many a patient. It is hardly a wonder that in the thirteenth and fourteenth centuries, Jews were doctors in numbers far exceeding their representation in the general populace. Only 5 percent of the twenty thousand people living in Marseilles during the first half of the fourteenth century were Jewish, for example, but they accounted for ten of the city's twenty-three physicians.

All of this was enhanced by the fact that so many Jewish doctors did, in fact, have special gifts, though they were not of the sort feared by so many of their patients. Not only did they bring with them the long tradition of Jewish healing, but the conditions in which they lived also contributed to their medical expertise. Era after era, Jews had been forced to flee from country to country, usually taking few of their possessions and often able to retain little of their money. Medical knowledge was not only transferable but, until licensing laws were established in various territories around the late eighteenth century, was a means of starting up an enterprise immediately upon arrival in a foreign place. Before the complexities of modern science began to overtake it in the early nineteenth century, it could be taught by father to son or within a community. Not permitted to own land until relatively recent times (and in any event unable to put it into a suitcase), Jews looked on medicine as a form of un-real estate, valued because of the very real conditions to which they had to respond realistically.

Traveling as they did, Jews learned many languages, and the medical men among them had contact with physicians from many areas, adding to their store of information and their comprehension of available texts, as well as enabling them to study the drugs used by local practitioners. In addition, the shared ability to speak and read Hebrew enabled them to transmit knowledge to one another. Their very privations added to their skills. Jews were of necessity cosmopolitan, and so was their medicine.

Ability with languages and the transmitted history of familiarity with the Hellenistic culture made the Jewish physician a valuable intermediary of Greek medicine—which continued to live as the scientific medicine of the Middle Ages and Renaissance—to the Christian and Arabic worlds. Not only were Jews among the translators of the ancient Greek texts into Arabic during the approximately six centuries when that language dominated medical thought, but they also produced versions in Hebrew, to be disseminated among themselves throughout Europe and the Muslim lands. Consequently, Jews had ready access to the most highly regarded of medical texts, which were generally unavailable to doctors on the Continent until the end of the twelfth century, if not later, when Latin translations were published, some of them by Jewish scholars. In fact, even the few Christian medical writings of this period were translated into Hebrew as well as Arabic, so Jewish doctors had access to everything then available in any literary form, whether emanating from Europe or from the Arab lands. It is hardly a wonder that more than a few Jews were members of the faculty of the first great university medical school, at Salerno, during the tenth, eleventh, and twelfth centuries. When the schools at Montpellier and Paris were established in the thirteenth century, Jewish physicians were called to teach there as well.

And always, there remained the religious basis upon which healing was so highly valued by Jews. When during the Middle Ages certain rabbinic authorities—threatened by the intellectual incursions of the sciences and philosophy— forbade the study of such matters, medicine was exempted because of the principle that life must be chosen, as God and the sages had decreed: the biblical dictum of *pikuah nefesh*, the ultimate value of saving a life. In 1305, for example, the threat of excommunication was imposed by the renowned Rabbi Solomon ben Adret (known as Rashba) on anyone who read in a scientific or philosophic discipline before the age of twenty-six, but learning medicine was allowed. And by then, the authority of Maimonides was being invoked to protect students of the sciences as well, as in a letter written to Rashba by another prominent rabbi, Jedaiah ben Abraham Bedersi (known as Penini). "We cannot give up science," he wrote. "It is in the breath of our nostrils. Even if Joshua were to appear and forbid it we would not obey him. For we have a warranty which outweighs them all, that is to say Maimonides, who recommended it and impressed it upon us. We are ready to set our goods, our children and our lives at stake for it." In these ways, not only medicine but science in general was vouchsafed as a valued outlet for Jewish intellectual energies.

And this was not the only exemption granted to Jewish doctors. Though church synods until well after the Renaissance frequently ordered Christians not to consult Jewish physicians, many of the ecclesiastical and royal dignitaries continued to have Jewish doctors, as did prominent families. In Spain, this situation persisted even after the Jews were expelled in 1492, including at the court of Ferdinand and Isabella. Not surprisingly, the medical entourage of late medieval and Renaissance popes more likely than not included one or more Jewish physicians.

The Jewish emphasis on maintaining health existed in the presence of a Christian abnegation of concerns with the body. The ascetic tradition, strong since the earliest days of the Church, meant that the truly religious must not only avoid the vanity of pursuing what is corporeal, but must also accept that disease is the work of the devil or a judgment from God, to be treated, if at all, by confession and prayer. The twelfth-century Saint Bernard, for example—

a man who seems to have gloried in being plagued throughout his life by chronic anemia and stomach problems—declared that monks who took medicines were in violation of Church precepts. In 1135, the Council of Rheims forbade monks and clergy from practicing medicine as contrary to theologic principles. Restrictions became even greater with succeeding councils, effectively shutting the profession off from participation by some of the most educated men of the time. More than one Church assembly threatened to excommunicate physicians who instituted treatment before requesting ecclesiastical consultation. Unlike the attitude of Jews, religious dogma pervaded Christian theories of sickness.

Christians fundamentally saw their existence on earth as mere preparation for the next world, regarding the body as no more than a container for the soul. Then, as always, Jews have lived for the time on earth, for the here and now, preserving health and this life as the way to understand God. Though believing in the eventual coming of the Messiah, they do not wait for redemption or salvation—they deal in a practical way with whatever is before them. Their interest is not in saving souls, but in saving lives. Jewish realism is a powerful factor in the Jewish determination to remain healthy and stave off death. Though the medieval Muslims called both Jews and Christians "the people of the book," Jews are in effect the people of the body as well.

It was Jewish realism that resulted in the building of institutions for the Jewish sick, as early as the Middle Ages but increasing markedly around the time of the Enlightenment. Living either in ghettos or confined by social pressure to specific areas of cities, their doctors usually restricted in the ability to treat in the hospitals that were beginning to appear in large numbers during the eighteenth century or to study in universities, Jews founded their own social service organizations under the leadership of community councils—among whose officers physicians figured prominently—that supported hospitals and sick-care societies, as well as other functions. Young Jewish men determined to learn the principles of the newly emerging scientific medicine were thus given the opportunity to work in the kinds of facilities that might not otherwise have been available to them or to their patients. The ancient Jewish proclivity to seek care, based originally on the biblical injunction to choose life but by then an almost ingrained personality characteristic, assured a large pool of patients. In these ways, restrictions that might have hindered professional development were countered by societal responses.

Jews, like everyone else, began to aspire to the middle class once that became possible. Just as the profession of medicine had brought entree into the courts of medieval monarchs and popes, it could make a Jew a member of the bourgeoisie after the Enlightenment. Particularly after the *Haskalah* of the late eighteenth century—the specifically Jewish Enlightenment when so many left the narrow intellectual confines of religious study to seek secular knowledge and acceptance—medicine was the ideal means to accomplish that objective, especially since the civil service, that other traditional stepping-stone to the middle class, was almost entirely closed to Jews.

Though particularly characteristic of the German community, the founding of Jewish health care institutions was a process that came into being in various forms throughout Europe. And so was the increasing attempt to burst out of the constricting confines of a totally religious perspective. As the universities became more accessible, the ancient Jewish emphasis on education began increasingly to be secularized, as a consequence of the *Haskalah*, and drew young Jews into classrooms and lecture halls as though to a magnet of worldly intellectualism. Jews became overrepresented at every grade, from primary school upward. To provide an example, although only 9 percent of the population of Vienna in 1912, Jews accounted for 47 percent of *gymnasium* students. The situation was almost as remarkable at higher levels: 25 percent of the students enrolled at the University of Vienna in 1904 were Jewish. Many of these were studying medicine.

For more than a generation, Jewish families had been pouring into the great capital city of Vienna from all parts of the Austro-Hungarian Empire, drawn by the relative liberalism of Emperor Franz-Joseph, and not deterred by political expressions of antisemitism that were everywhere rampant. As they freed themselves from the confining religious environment of the small cities and villages in which they had been brought up, parents did what they could to secure for their children the advantages of the surrounding society. In no area was this phenomenon more pronounced than in the study of medicine.

The situation alarmed some of the most prominent figures in German academic medicine. Theodor Billroth, the leading surgical professor at the university's General Hospital of Vienna in the late nineteenth century, railed against the presence of such large numbers of newly arrived Jewish immigrants in his classes. He described his view of the problem in *The Medical Sciences in the German Universities*, a book destined to become a classic of educational philosophy throughout the world.

No profession, except perhaps, the clergy, is so often exploited by uneducated families who aim to climb into the cultured classes on the shoulders of the younger generation, as is the medical profession. For the Jews, a medical career offers comparatively fewer difficulties than any other, and if a doctor once achieves moderate success, countless others will attempt to duplicate it. . . .

A Jewish merchant in Galicia or Hungary (the Hungarian Jews have the worst reputation among the Viennese students themselves), earning just enough to keep himself and his family from starving, has a moderately gifted son. The vanity of the mother demands a scholar, a Talmudist, in the family. . . . He comes to Vienna with his clothes and nothing else. What impressions, what stimuli can such a boy have received?

He has been surrounded all his life by the pettiest and most miserable circumstances, nor will he ever be able to rid himself of this narrowest of horizons. Now he comes to the university. . . .[O]ur teaching methods were not intended for such students, or for such conditions, for those methods demand a free mind and free intellectual movement. Such people are in no way fitted for a scientific career.

And this was written by a man of broad liberal outlook, generally conceded to have been among the most tolerant of the German-speaking professors of the day. Among the reasons his words had wide appeal was that they did, in fact, reflect certain truths about Jewish medical aspirations in a Christian society, some of which have never disappeared— nor would any Jew want them to. But, almost certainly unappreciated by all but a few of Billroth's readers, they also reflected some of the conditions under which Jews in every era and land have striven toward careers in medicine, not only for the immediate reasons given by Billroth, but for those far more sweeping and all-inclusive historical reasons.

Though the association of Jews with medicine that consolidated during the early Middle Ages was based on religious precepts and cultural ambience, the centuries have interlarded another factor, which is as universal as it is personal. By this I mean a characteristic that can only be called the Jewish personality. In this era of extreme sensitivity to such notions as ethnic and national characteristics, some might think it preferable to use more euphemistic terms like *worldview*, *philosophical outlook*, and *cultural orientation*, but they all amount to the same thing. The Jewish attitude toward life and the world has certain qualities that have been remarked upon for centuries, by observers both friendly and hostile; stereotypes, of whatever group, do sometimes persist because they support personal impressions. Though some of such impressions are only what the beholder wants to see, some of them are true observations, in the sense of having validity to objective minds. Among those that have been made about Jews, several would seem to bear on the questions posed at the outset of this chapter, which can be summarized by asking, "What is it about the Jews and medicine?"

Among Jews, especially those of an intellectual bent, there is commonly a kind of restlessness, an anticipation of uncertainty, ambiguity, imperfection and the sense that one must do something about it even though the total solution will never be found. Many have lived in relative comfort with a chronic sense of discomfort. Irritability and a persistent low-grade aggravation are in the very marrow of such people. Though these qualities rankle, they may be the source of an active response to the world, whether productive or counterproductive. As the sociologist Thorstein Veblen famously put it in his frequently quoted essay of 1919, *The Intellectual Pre-eminence of Jews in Modern Europe*, "They are neither a complaisant nor a contented lot, these aliens of the uneasy feet."

Out of this restless dissatisfaction there arises a skepticism, a questioning of oneself, of one's place in the predom-
inantly Christian world and, indeed, of the givens of that
world, both great and small. Many Jews have felt themselves
less bound by the encompassing assumptions of the surrounding culture, in part because they could never be wholly
a part of it. "The first requisite for constructive work in
modern science, and indeed for any work of inquiry that
shall bring enduring results, is a skeptical frame of mind,"
Veblen correctly pointed out. What, indeed, is the practice
of medicine, and what is the science upon which it is based,
but exercises in applied skepticism, a dissatisfaction with
the direction in which things are going, and a determination
to do something about it, even though the doing may of
necessity remain incomplete? So ancient is the restlessness
to get under way with the undertaking that it was already
being articulated in the first century C.E. by Rabbi Tarfon, a
sage quoted in the *Pirkei Avot* of the Mishnah as saying, "It is
not your duty to complete the work, but neither are you free
to desist from it."

Modern Jews often approach their work in the same way
as did the Talmudists who preceded them by a millennium
and a half: by focusing on details, by applying a questioning
eye to the most minute annoyances and inconsistencies in
their lives and in their fields of vision. They ruminate and
lucubrate on such seemingly small things, and never stop
turning them over in their minds. The very closeness of

their grievances with the presumed order demands a closeness of scrutiny.

Does any of this sound familiar? It should, because it is the way of the scientist and the way of the physician. From the specific to the general, proclaim the advocates of the inductive reasoning that has been the boon of science; use the general principles to explain the tiniest details of observations and disorders, say the advocates of the deductive reasoning that is the key to diagnostic and therapeutic medicine. When the Nazis called psychoanalytic theory "the Jewish science," they were expressing, far better than they knew, the debt that Sigmund Freud owed to the meticulous cogitations of his Talmudic forebears. Though psychoanalysis is hardly a science, it derived its scrutinizing methodology from Freud's training in the laboratory, as he sought to interpret minutely the laws of nature as they applied to neurophysiology. And I would submit that it derived its distinctively Freudian viewpoint from Freud's unconscious absorption of the ancient rabbinic tradition—knowingly and unknowingly transmitted by his own Talmudically steeped father—of painstakingly interpreting the laws of God as they apply to daily living. As much as Jews are the people of the book and the people of the body, they are the people of transmitted memory. *L 'dor va-dor*, says the liturgy, "from generation to generation." Conscious or not, the ways of medical thinking are in the Jewish psyche.

And now it is necessary to return to the words of the

*Geheimrat*, Theodor Billroth. Many jokes are made about the Jewish mother who boasts about "my son, the doctor." But viewed in the perspective of millennia of history, of a tradition ultimately based on the search for knowledge of God, of a society that has valued learning almost as much as it values life—and, indeed, perceives learning as the high road to life and therefore to God—is it any wonder that such a society would hold the practice of healing to be the greatest good, and therefore to hold those who practice it in greatest esteem? Only the Talmudist has stood higher than the *rofe* in the calculus of Jewish honor, and in early times the two were frequently embodied in the same person. Several centuries ago, the religious intellectualism of the rabbi began to be replaced by the secular intellectualism of the doctor, and that process has grown and now dominates Jewish thinking. The *rav* has become the *docere*.

# Spain–Morocco–Egypt

> When a man finds it arduous to gain a livelihood in
> one country, he emigrates to another. All the more is
> it incumbent upon a Jew who is restricted in the
> practice of his religion to depart for another place.
>
> —MOSES MAIMONIDES,
> *Letter to Yemen*

This has been the history of the Jewish people since the
Diaspora began after the destruction of the First Temple in 586 B.C.E. Though actual captivity—as by the Babylo-
nians, the Romans, or the Nazis—has been rare, the need to
emigrate has existed in every era. Whether to save his life, to
protect his subsistence, or to avoid being "restricted in the
practice of his religion," the Jew has frequently found it necessary to "depart for another place."

And so it was in 1148 for Rabbi Maimon ben Joseph, a
*dayyan*, or judge of the rabbinical court of Cordoba, when he
gathered his family about him in preparation for a hegira

whose ultimate goal he was not destined to reach. Maimon's family consisted of his second wife, their one-year-old child, David, and the rabbi's ten-year-old son, Moses. Maimon's first wife had died shortly after giving birth to Moses on the afternoon of the eve of Passover, 4898, or March 30, 1138, in the Gregorian calendar. (Until recent scholarship discovered otherwise, most biographers had recorded 4895 and 1135 as the correct years.) There were also two daughters, of whom little is known save that the younger of them was named Miriam. The Cordoba they were leaving was undergoing alarming transformations, by which not only religious freedom but life itself was being put into peril. The period so often called the golden age of Spain was rapidly coming to an end for the Cordobans after four centuries of glory; the reverberations of its crashing demise threatened a Jewish community that had long lived in productive harmony with its Muslim and Christian neighbors.

Following the Muslim invasion of the Iberian peninsula in the early eighth century, a civilization had gradually arisen there that became the envy of Western capitals, and Cordoba under the Umayyad sect was its center, with a caliphate said to rival that of Baghdad. By the beginning of the tenth century, Cordobans had good reason to be convinced that their city was the cultural hub of the known universe, or, as the city was called by an emissary of the Holy Roman Emperor Otto I, "the ornament of the world." Though the fall of the caliphate to a rival sect in the early eleventh century lessened the city's authority and influence, it was still a vibrant and beautiful place a century later, estimated by historians to have been home to more than 100,000 Muslims, Jews, and Christians, all with some level of citizenship and all with equal access to the libraries, hospitals, marketplaces, baths, observatories, and well-kept public spaces that characterized it.

Most important for the Jews was the fact that as the "people of the Book," they and Christians were granted the status of *dhimmis*, those who were protected by Koranic law and allowed to practice their religion in recognition of submitting to Muslim authority. But protection does not mean equality, and tolerance is different from full participation. There were distinctions of privilege and access sufficiently restrictive that it has become customary to refer, and correctly so, to the "second-class" status of the *dhimmi*. Still, released from the deprivations they had endured under the Visigoths, the Jews thrived and became a prosperous community whose members made important contributions to the political, economic, and cultural life of the peninsula. Like the inhabitants of all the cities of Andalusia—southernmost Spain—the people of Cordoba were thoroughly Arabized. In dress, language, and popular culture, it was difficult to distinguish one group from another. Jews and Christians wrote Arabic poetry, composed and played Arabic music, and served in the Arabic government, sometimes in high positions. Although most of the Jews seem to have lived in one area, the so-called Juderia, this was by choice rather than fiat, just as certain neighborhoods of prominent cities today are still known as ethnic enclaves.

No Cordoban was more the beneficiary of the atmosphere of tolerance and religious freedom than Rabbi Maimon. Although the source of his income is uncertain, it is known that he was able to live well, in a comfortable, book-filled house of the Moorish style. The seventh generation of leaders of the Jewish community of Spain, he has been said (though erroneously and never claimed by himself) to have traced his family tree to Rabbi Judah ha-Nasi, who was the first to compile the ancient Oral Law of the Jews and present it in a written form, called the Mishnah, near the end of the second century C.E. A putative descendant of King David, Judah's title of ha-Nasi, or Prince, had meant that he was the presiding judge of the Sanhedrin and the undisputed leader of the Jewish community in Palestine. Like Judah, Maimon was considered to be the outstanding scholar of religious law in his country, and was at the same time skilled in mathematics and astronomy, as befit a well-educated man of that time and place. According to legend, Maimon's first wife—the mother of Moses—was the daughter of an uneducated butcher, whom he was instructed in a dream to marry. Though virtually nothing is known of his second wife, David's mother, she is thought to have come from a family whose station was more like her husband's.

Young Moses was educated primarily by his father, though he had other tutors as well. Being a precocious boy, he learned not only Jewish law and history but also such subjects as philosophy, rhetoric, astronomy, science, and mathematics, and seems to have pored over his father's medical books as well. As for so many intellectually gifted students of the medieval period, the goal set for him was to master all knowledge.

At the beginning, the path was not easy. As a young child, Moses was an indifferent and uncaring student despite his father's determined efforts. Unresponsive to Maimon's encouragement, cajoling, and finally his ire and punishments, the boy is said—in one of the colorful legends that have grown up around the early life of the Rambam—to have frequently sneaked off to seek refuge in the empty women's section of the synagogue, where no one would think to look for him on any weekday morning or afternoon. There he would lament his tribulations to God, praying for some relief from the failure that some must have attributed to his having been the offspring of an unlearned butcher's daughter. As his childhood progressed without evidence of improvement, even the child's father is said to have given up any hope that he would change. It is part of the legend that Maimon at one point lost his patience sufficiently to blurt out harsh words that must have devastated the sensitive Moses. "You were born for the lowest levels of life!" he roared, and the lad cringed.

Legend—for much of what has been recounted of Moses's early life is legend, sometimes merging into myth—has it that the boy impulsively took flight from his father's house on hearing this pronouncement, which must have sounded to his young ears like an immutable judgment. Repeated anxious searches by the family and many members of the community failed to discover his whereabouts, and it was feared that he would never again be seen.

Several years passed, and the conscience-stricken Maimon tried to become reconciled to the loss of his son, burying himself in studies and in writing tractates on the Torah and Talmudic literature. And then one day, a seeming miracle occurred. At the end of a regular service, the men of the great synagogue of Cordoba found themselves enthralled with a brilliant rabbinic discourse being delivered in the voice of a youth barely beyond young childhood, whose face was covered by the prayer shawl enfolded around his head and shoulders in a manner not unusual for those lecturing on holy matters before the congregation. As the address concluded amid the admiring murmurings of the assembled company, the very young man drew the prayer shawl from his face, revealing himself to be none other than Moses, the prodigal son of Rabbi Maimon. He could not have been older than ten.

This is another of those pretty stories, and elements of it may well be similar to the actual events. Those convinced of its truth never make reference to the unlikelihood of a boy wearing a prayer shawl before he has reached the age of bar mitzvah, or, in fact, to the improbability that any of these events really took place. And yet, as apocryphal as its details must be, the tale continues to be told for reasons beyond those of teller and listeners merely wanting it to be true. It is repeated endlessly because it is consistent with everything known not only about the brilliance of the young Moses after his transformation, but about his ability to absorb vast amounts of difficult material in short periods of time, and even at that young age to possess the driving ambition to learn and to interpret, which would characterize him for the rest of his life.

Another version of the tale has it that Maimon became so frustrated with trying to teach his son that he finally gave up the attempt and sent him away to live with his own teacher, Rabbi Joseph ibn Migas, a prominent scholar who was one of the most important figures in the evolution of Spanish Talmudism. Those who tell it this way assert that the episode in the synagogue occurred following a few years of concentrated study under the tutelage of the older man. With only minor variations, this scenario seems likely to have been closer to the actual course of events—if indeed any of it really took place.

What is known for certain is that it was a comfortable, secure existence that Rabbi Maimon's family had been living up to the time they were forced to flee Cordoba. There had been no political reason for apprehension or concern. After so long a period of harmony within a Muslim state, it had seemed as though life could go on like this forever. But it all ended with a shocking swiftness in 1148, when the peninsula came under the control of the Almohads, a violent fundamentalist Muslim sect originating among the Berbers of North Africa, under the leadership of their fanatical chief,

Abdallah ibn Tumart. Jewish and Christian schools were closed, churches and synagogues were destroyed, and non-Muslims given the option of conversion or death; emigration was forbidden for fear that the refugees might be of aid to rival leaders. Many of the Jews undertook a sort of pseudo-conversion, made easier by the fact that the Almohads only demanded public observance, such as occasional attendance at the mosque, and paid little attention to what was done in the privacy of homes. But this was a compromise that Rabbi Maimon was not willing to make. Leaving behind the belongings of generations of his family—including all but a few books from his vast library—he escaped into exile with his wife and four children.

Maimon's first destination was the Mediterranean port city of Almeria in southeastern Spain, not yet occupied by the Almohads. It was on this journey, undertaken in the company of a group of other fleeing Jewish families, that the pattern was set by which young Moses would continue the education he had begun, whether he had accomplished it on his own as portrayed in the two forms of the legend or with the advantage of his father's library. Teachers were somehow always found during the arduous pilgrimage to uncertain destinations, books were constantly being borrowed and exchanged with other learned Jews, and Maimon oversaw every aspect of his gifted son's instruction, conducting much of it himself. The makeshift pedagogical process was aided by the boy's prodigious ability to absorb large quantities of information and to remember it without notes, a fortunate gift on which he would comment in later years. "The forgetfulness that befalls men has never befallen me in my youth," he wrote. Once read, the contents of entire books seem to have remained in his memory.

In Almeria, a friendship is thought to have developed between Moses and the son of a Muslim judge, who was a political refugee from Cordoba. Though this young man, Averroës (Abu al-Walid Muhammad ibn Muhammad ibn Rushd, in the original Arabic), was nine years older than his Jewish companion, they would have found much to discuss, especially in view of Averroës's burgeoning interest in finding a concordance between Greek thought and Islamic belief. He would go on to become one of the most influential of the Arabic philosophers, writing tracts on the works of Aristotle and Plato that would influence Christian, Muslim, and Jewish commentators for centuries to come, as did those that Moses would later produce. Averroës had not fled to Almeria to escape the Almohads—he would, in fact, spend most of his life serving under them as chief judge of Cordoba and personal physician to several caliphs—but because he had written a commentary on the Koran that was considered too liberal, necessitating his temporary absence from the city of his birth. Like so many other of the details of Maimonides' life at this early time, there is no certainty that he ever did actually meet Averroës, although more than a few biographers write of the relationship as though it had definitely taken place.

Maimon's family left Almeria in 1151, when the Almohads entered it as conquerors. They seemed to have wandered from town to town during the next eight or nine years, unable to leave Spain until 1160, when emigration was permitted following ibn Tumart's death. Taking ship to Morocco, they settled in Fez. During all that time of Andalusian homelessness, Maimon had seen to it that Moses's education was never interrupted. And Moses did the same for his brother, David, who became his pupil and his younger companion. If misfortune and uncertainty breed strong qualities of character, this was doubtless the period of the older son's maturation, when he learned to cope with the difficulties that would later assail him in so many aspects of his life. Although his solidarity with the Jewish community formed from his earliest years, his experiences during these times of homelessness, when the family's safety—and probably their very subsistence—could come only from the Jews they encountered on their journeys, must have intensified that ever-growing closeness and intense loyalty to his people.

Incredibly, young Moses somehow found time to write during the period of restless and often dangerous travel. Initiating a pattern of ceaseless literary activity that would characterize his scholarship for the rest of his life, his rapidly maturing intellect produced a short treatise on the language of logic and metaphysics, commentaries on a few sections of the Bible, and an essay on the Jewish calendar involving rather complex mathematical and astronomical calculations, at the age of not much more than twenty. In

1158, during the family's penultimate year in Spain, he began work on a commentary on the Mishnah that would take him ten years to complete. His aim was to produce a work that was understandable to the common man, whose knowledge of biblical and Talmudic literature was not great. Writing in Arabic using the Hebrew alphabet, as was the custom among Jewish authors in Muslim countries at the time—a style that would later become known as Judeao-Arabic—he called his book *Siraj*, meaning "luminous light," a title that suggested the motivation of so much of his writings, to elucidate concepts that might be abstruse to the average man.

The need for a redaction of the Mishnah seemed obvious to Moses. The laws by which Jews lived—in aggregate called halakha—were based on interpretation of biblical writ. These interpretations had been originally promulgated by generations of rabbinical commentaries and decisions, and passed down orally, either by individual authorities or by the teachings in academies. Because the laws had never been assembled into a written book, there were discrepancies between the teachings committed to memory by succeeding individuals or taught in schools. Around 200 C.E., Judah ha-Nasi, the Patriarch of the Jewish community in the land of Israel, undertook to compile the divergent mass of oral tradition, codifying it into a single consistent text, the Mishnah, meaning "learning by repetition." Judah divided the laws of the Mishnah into six general sections, containing a total of sixty-three tractates, each of which was further divided into chapters.

In the following several centuries, approximately 200–500 C.E., rabbinic discussions and musings on the Mishnah were compiled together with records of judicial halakhic decisions into a text called the Gemara, which was meant to be a supplement to the earlier book, taking a more generalized and thoughtful approach to the underlying truths of Jewish belief. In essence, the Gemara is a commentary on the Mishnah, but with a difference: Whereas the Mishnah provides what is essentially a utilitarian halakhic guide to living, the Gemara is more a bouillabaisse of wide-ranging legalistic discussions and folklore as derived from the teachings of the Torah, whether or not the subject under discussion has any practical application. Though the vast majority of its contents derive from the time after the compilation of the Mishnah, it also refers to the teachings of a few authors not included in the Mishnah.

The separate communities of Palestine and Babylon each produced its own Gemara, which, though based on the same Mishnah, are in fact quite different. But they do have a similar general form. In both, a precept of the Mishnah is followed on the page by the record of a rabbinic discussion that is a mixture of legal argumentation, legend, and story-telling. That part—representing between two thirds and three quarters of the text and not being halakha—is called *aggadah*, and is intended to illustrate or illuminate the matter under consideration. The discussions may drift from the original topic, but always return to it in spite of numerous tangents. The Gemara transcends time in the sense that the commentary of multiple scholars of succeeding centuries (the most prominent of whom would later be the eleventh-century French rabbi Rashi) were later inserted in the margins of the page so as to surround the Mishnah passage and original commentary of the sages of the third to sixth centuries, thus adding to the complexity of the debates and the length of the total text. The word *Talmud*, or "teaching," is the name given to the collection of books that is the Mishnah plus the Gemara, though the word is frequently used to indicate only the latter.

Because the Gemara was compiled long after the Mishnah, correct understanding of halakha demanded in-depth study of the more recent book's intricacies, a daunting prospect to any but the most dedicated scholars. Moses determined to produce a compendium making use of only the most essential Talmudic precepts, thereby permitting direct access to an understanding of the Mishnah for less learned readers, or for those who simply did not have the time or inclination to wade through the vastly more complicated, abstruse, and disorganized text of the Gemara. He had two other goals as well: One was to provide for his readers an easy introduction to the Talmud; the other was to restore his putative ancestor's great work as a primary source from which the Jewish law might be understood. Judah ha-Nasi's text would once again stand by itself as an independent compilation of the Law. This undertaking, Moses's commentary on the Mishnah, would take him ten years to complete.

By the time the young scholar began his project, it was becoming increasingly obvious that the kind of intellectual work to which Moses was dedicating his efforts was not consistent with his family's unsettled and migratory existence. More books were needed than could be obtained easily, and he had to be in contact on a regular basis with scholars with whom ideas might be exchanged. In essence, the family had been in hiding—perhaps hiding not only themselves but their Jewishness too—since leaving Cordoba, and such a state of affairs was hardly conducive to a continued high level of unharried thought and literary undertakings. The Maimons needed to be in a Jewish community more stable than those they had encountered on their precarious ramblings from one Andalusian town to another. As much as they sought such stability, they must also have yearned for a place where no Muslim would know that they were Jewish, in order to observe their rituals in a secrecy more certain than had been possible during their dangerous wanderings. For these reasons, Maimon decided to take his family to the Moroccan city of Fez, where the persecution of Jews by the Almohads was at least as bad as it had been in Spain, but which provided certain advantages not obtainable on the road or in the Iberian towns.

Unlike some of the places in which the family had hidden, Fez still had secular schools where a wide variety of subjects were taught that Moses wanted to explore in more depth, such as mathematics, astronomy, philosophy, and the natural sciences. Having studied some medicine in his youth, he wanted the opportunity to learn more by associating with skilled physicians. And so, though Fez was a city from which some Jewish families were fleeing, to the Maimons it seemed an intellectual haven.

But when they arrived, they were disappointed to find the Jewish community in a state of spiritual torpor, well beyond the mere fearfulness to which they had long been accustomed. Though the family expected to find repression similar to what they had experienced in Cordoba under the Almohads, they could not have been prepared for the mood of pessimism and spiritual confusion that awaited them in Morocco. The fundamentalist sect conquered Fez in 1145, and the inhabitants of the city had been suffering under their terrifying rule for fifteen years. Some Jews had emigrated and some had converted, but most had chosen to utter the Muslim formula for conversion and outwardly conform to Islam while secretly adhering—clinging, actually—to Jewish belief and practice. Many of them were losing heart, however, or had already done so. After this long period of outward conformity to the precepts of their conquerors, there were those among them who were beginning to question the basis of their own faith, specifically whether the newer religion to which they had sworn obedience was not in fact meant to be the successor to their own. Perhaps God had intended it this way, that Muhammad's truth was greater than the truth of their own lawgiver, Moses. And perhaps Muhammad was indeed more authoritative, as they had been forced to concede when they recited the words that saved their lives: "There is no God but Allah, and Muhammad is His prophet."

Matters had been made worse by a letter recently received from a prominent rabbi who had fled Morocco to settle in a foreign country. The letter was written in response to a request that had come from a local man, for his opinion of the way in which the Jews of the area were living, hiding the truth of their rituals and acting as though fully assimilated into the religious life of their Muslim neighbors. The rabbi, living safely in a far-off place, had replied with a vitriolic denunciation of the Jews of Fez, whom he assailed as heathens regardless of their prayers and supplications to the ancient God of Israel. Such prayers, he declaimed, were the refuge of hypocrites and unbelievers. Those offering them should not be considered Jews, for if this sort of behavior were to become common, Judaism would soon be extinct.

Rabbi Maimon could not allow such a condemnation to remain unanswered. In 1160, shortly after arriving in Fez, he wrote an open letter to the Jews of Morocco, reassuring them that they were still members of their people, and still favored by God in the ancient covenant between God and Israel. Maimon reiterated that the outward appearance of Muslim practice is justified for the sake of survival, but it is inward faith that is the true test of a Jew. Prayers must continue to be recited, he wrote in the fervent epistle that became known as the *Letter of Consolation*, even if they were silent and heard only by God and one's heart.

It was his heart, in fact, from which Maimon's letter
came. But when his son wrote another epistle two years
later, it came from the younger man's cerebral, logical head.
The intent of the *Letter on Conversion* (in Hebrew, *Iggeret ha-
Shemad*) that Moses wrote in 1162 was to convince his coreligionists that the emigré rabbi's words of denunciation were
inconsistent not only with the Law but with the history of
Judaism as well. As though to assert his authority from the
outset, the young scholar began his peroration with the
forceful announcement "Here speaks Moses, son of Maimon
the Judge, the Spaniard," using the full name that would in
the Renaissance come to be rendered as Maimonides in the
manner of the Greeks. Such opening sentences constituted a
stylistic form commonly employed by pamphleteers of the
time, and he knew it well. He also was familiar with the
metaphorical usages of the period, though it may be significant that he chose the field of medicine from which to take
them, writing: "When I recognized the astonishing facts of
the case, which is like an illness of the eyes, I resolved to
gather herbs and elixirs from the writings of the ancients
and to compound an eye ointment that would prevail against
this illness. With God's help, I will therefore heal the
disease."

The letter went on to cite Talmudic passages confirming
that one is permitted to save his own life by disguising
himself in times of persecution, and told of the stratagems
used in the past by leading rabbis to convince Roman soldiers that they were not Jews. At various times in history,

Maimonides reminded his readers, idols had been worshipped and other seeming desecrations had been performed, always with exoneration when the eventual return
took place. Even the Talmudic sages Rabbi Meir and Rabbi
Eleazar had feigned heathenism to save themselves. Not only
were the Jews of Fez justified in what they were doing,
Moses reassured them, but they would be rewarded by God
for enduring their pseudo-conversion as they did. Anyone
who condemned them was not merely misguided but unbal-
anced. "Are they healthy, these fanatics who express such an
opinion," he questioned, "or mentally sick?"

Throughout his life, Moses would advocate departure
from a country where Jews could not practice their religion
openly. But in Fez, he recognized from his own experience
that emigration was impossible for some people, or at least
extremely difficult. In such situations, he counseled, the
most important duty was to avoid profaning the name of
God. Men were to pray when possible, in any way that was
possible, but beyond that he sanctioned the widest latitude
for survival. "We are not asked to render service to heathenism," he wrote in the letter, "but only to recite an
empty formula which the Muslims themselves know we
utter insincerely in order to circumvent a bigot. . . . If a man
asks me, 'Shall I be slain or utter the formula of Islam?,'
I answer, 'Utter the formula and live.' " Moreover, he rea-
soned, since the Muslims worshipped the same God as did
the Jews and called Muhammad a prophet and not a deity,
the public professing of Islam was less of a burden than

Christianity—considered to be idolatry—and this, too, must be taken into account.

The vehemence with which Maimonides defended the pseudo-converts has given rise to much speculation through the centuries. It is generally agreed that Maimon's family showed no outward sign of being Jewish while in Fez. Moses himself used the name abu Imran Musa ibn Maimon during this period, the name by which he would later be called in Arabic medical and philosophical literature. Subterfuge was abetted by the city's construction: Its houses were for the most part concealed behind high walls, the streets were narrow and dark, and it was possible to go unrecognized even by people to whom one was well known, especially because the Almohads demanded that faces be partially covered in public. It is not unlikely that the men of the family took the Muslim oath of conversion and did, in fact, behave in every one of the ways that Maimon and Moses were addressing in their respective tractates. It is impossible to know how far they went in their deception, and some have suggested that they may have exceeded their neighbors, going well beyond what was absolutely necessary. Certain Arabic sources of the time, in fact, claim that they practiced Islam openly.

No justification is needed for the letter that the prominent sage Rabbi Maimon wrote to reassure the Jews of Fez. But one may ask why his son, only twenty-four years old and not yet a well-known scholar, felt called upon to do the same two years later. The letter is so strongly worded, even tinged at certain points with sarcasm, that some have wondered why Moses took such an extreme tack. Was it to rationalize his own actions or, even more extremely put, to lay down a smoke screen of self-justification behind which to hide the reality of how far he had moved from the essence of his faith during the time of his family's travels in Spain and its sojourn in Fez? Had Moses himself, in fact, at some point briefly become fully Muslim in the same way that so many Jews have pragmatically embraced Christianity in recent centuries?

These are not questions with ready answers, and perhaps they have no answers at all, or at least none that will ever be known. And they are asked not in an attempt to denigrate the man but to understand him. Maimonides would devote so much of the intellectual effort of his life to striving toward an integration of the teachings of Aristotle with the Law of the Jews that more than a few students of his life have wondered where his heart actually lay—with the Law or with philosophy—and how open he was to the possibility that halakha was too restrictive to allow a dispassionate and thoroughly objective interpretation of the natural world and the phenomena of human behavior. If there is a single factor that characterizes his thought, it is the constant seeking to observe and interpret the world as it really is, and to find a place for his conclusions within the realm of received Law. These are matters to which this narrative will return in later chapters.

The city of Fez during those years was suffused with suffering and danger. The repression that existed under the local caliph Abd al-Mumin worsened when he died in 1163 and was replaced by an even more severe tyrant, Abu Yakub Yusuf. Matters came to a head for the Maimons two years later, when the leading rabbi of the city, Judah ibn Shoshan—a pseudo-convert like virtually all Jews there—was seized and charged with reverting to the practice of Judaism, a crime for which he was tortured and killed by the Muslim authorities. Judah's presence was one of the primary reasons that the family had moved to Fez, and he had fulfilled their expectations of friendship by providing Moses with books needed for his studies and by introducing him to Jewish and Muslim scholars with whom he could continue his education in both secular and religious matters. Moses himself is said to have also been arrested at about this time, saved only by the intervention of Abul Arab ibn Moisha, a Muslim poet and theologian who risked his own life to help a valued friend. But even ibn Moisha did not know the truth—he believed in the sincerity of that friend's conversion. After five years of hiding the true nature of their beliefs, the time had come for the Maimons to leave Fez.

The family had had enough of the tyrannies of the Almohads. Moreover, Moses was by then a marked man; it seemed only a matter of time before the truth was revealed and he would once again be taken into custody. Maimon determined to take ship to Palestine, conquered by Crusaders in 1099 and now known as the Kingdom of Jerusalem. As difficult as living under Christian rule might prove to be, it was necessary to get far away from the threat under which his family lived in Muslim lands.

Maimonides' attitude toward Christians was that they were idolaters. They venerated images of Jesus, Mary, and a variety of saints, unlike the Muslims, who worshipped the same universal God as the Jews. Not only that, but the Jews of Jerusalem had been massacred, along with Muslims, as recently as 1148 by soldiers of the Second Crusade. There was plenty of reason for animosity and even contempt to be added to the trepidation that the travelers must have felt as they planned their escape to the Holy Land.

Because the family was by this time under surveillance, it was necessary to depart Fez under cover of darkness, which the Maimons did just after Passover, on April 18, 1165. Throughout their journey toward the sea, they would hide during the day and walk as far as they could after night fell. Other than immediate necessities, they had once again left behind everything they owned except a few books and the gemstones in which David and Moses had begun to trade, all of the Maimons' small supply of money having gone into their purchase.

The Maimons arrived late one night at the port city of Ceuta, where they hid from the authorities until being able to book passage on a ship to Acre. They left in the month of Iyar (coinciding with May) and arrived at their destination approximately a month later. But the voyage was far from uneventful. Six days out to sea, the ship was overtaken by a huge storm that threatened to capsize it. In later years, Maimonides would describe his response to the danger:

> On the evening of the first day of the week, the fourth of the month of Iyar, I went to sea, and on Sabbath the tenth of Iyar, of the four thousand nine hundred and twenty fifth year of the creation, we had a dreadful storm; the sea was in a fury and we were in danger of perishing. Then I vowed to keep these two days as complete fast days for myself and my household, and all those connected with me, and to command my children to do the same throughout all their generations; they should also give to charity according to their ability. For myself I further vowed to remain apart from human intercourse on every tenth of Iyar, to speak to nobody and only to pray and to study, as on that day I saw no one on the sea except the Holy One, praised be his name, so will I see no one and stay with no one on that day in the years to come. On the evening of the first day of the week, the 3rd day of Sivan, I landed safely and came to Acre, and by arriving in the land of Israel, I escaped persecution. This day I vowed to keep as a day of rejoicing, festivity and distribution of charity, for myself and my house throughout all generations.

(It appears that Miriam did not accompany the three men to Acre. There is some further record of the older girl, who remained with the family until marrying a Jewish scribe in the Egyptian court, around 1175. A letter by Miriam to Maimonides from a much later time has been found, in which she complains that her son, at that time living in a far-off land, never writes to her.)

The Acre in which the Maimons found themselves was a bustling metropolis with the largest Jewish community in Palestine, but "largest" meant only two hundred families. Fears of Christian persecution proved to be unfounded. The ruling knightly orders, having realized that they needed the economic and perhaps the cultural benefits brought by the presence of non-Christians, permitted civil freedoms throughout the Kingdom of Jerusalem. But, in fact, not many Jews had availed themselves of the opportunity to settle there. Once arrived, Moses was able to study the unchanged religious forms of the few Jews who had dwelt in Palestine since earliest times, causing him to modify some of his own customs. But in distinction to his usual easy relationships with Muslim colleagues, he seems to have avoided any attempt to make contact with Christians, keeping himself at a distance because of his sense that they were idolaters and nonbelievers in the unity of God.

When the summer had passed, the Maimons spent three days in the city of Jerusalem to contemplate the holy sites, with which their studies and their prayers had made them so familiar that they felt at home among them. As there was no organized community of Jews in Jerusalem, the time they spent in the city must have been disappointing, except for the opportunity to pray at such revered places as the

Western Wall. The men then went on to Hebron in order to visit the cave of Machpelah, in which the patriarchs and matriarchs—Abraham, Isaac, and Jacob; Sarah, Rebecca, and Leah—are buried. Maimonides has left an account of this brief period of pilgrimage, in which he echoes the hopes of so many who visited those places before him and those countless thousands who came there in the centuries preceding the founding of the State of Israel:

> I entered the great and holy place and prayed there on the sixth of the same month. On the first day of the following week, being the ninth, I left Jerusalem and went to Hebron, in order to kiss the graves of the patriarchs in the cave. On that day I stood in the cave and prayed: Thanks be to the father of all for everything! The two days, the sixth and ninth of Marheshvan [October, roughly] I designated by a vow as festivals devoted to solemn prayer and festivity. May God give me strength and assist me to fulfill my vows; and may I and all Israel soon be permitted to see the land in its glory, even as I prayed there, in its state of desolation! Amen.

Palestine was a disappointment. It was indeed a desolate land, with only small numbers of forlorn and generally impoverished Jews except for the few who were itinerant merchants or entrepreneurs. It bustled with the presence of Christians who had come because of religious zealotry, the lure of opportunity, or to serve as mercenaries in the various armed groups that seemed to be everywhere, behaving more like brigands than soldiers of the Cross. Moreover, it had become a refuge for the worst kind of escapees from ordinary society: thieves, prostitutes, gamblers, and those running away from retribution for their misdeeds. It was not the place for a serious scholar of Judaism, philosophy, and science: It was not the place for a man who would one day write:

> It is in the nature of man to orient himself in his character and actions according to his friends and companions and the practices of his compatriots. Hence, a man must associate with the righteous and always dwell with the wise, in order to learn from their ways of life. He must, however, stay aloof from the wicked, who walk in darkness, so that he will not learn from their actions. For whosoever frequents the wise becomes wise, but whosoever is a companion of the wicked will become wicked himself. If a man lives in a place whose customs are repugnant and whose inhabitants do not walk in the right path, he must migrate to a place whose inhabitants are pious and have good morals.

Compared to the lands through which Maimonides had passed, conditions for the Jews of Egypt were far superior. Not only did they live in relative freedom and stability, but some families had achieved a degree of prosperity. The attraction was great, especially for itinerants who had suffered so much. Taking ship once more at Acre, the family set out on what would prove to be the final leg of their long journey from home. They were on their way to a measure of liberty, ironically to be found in the place where their ancestors had lived in slavery and persecution.

# The *Commentary on the Mishnah*

That the ancient land of bondage should now be the
country in which Jews enjoyed the greatest measure of
freedom was an irony that must have occupied Moses's mind
as he and his family boarded one of the huge vessels—called
Alexandrians for their home port—that would take them to
Egypt. Alexandria, in fact, was their destination.

*The Itinerary of Benjamin of Tudela*, a book written by a
peripatetic rabbi and merchant who visited Jewish communities in Europe and as far away as the western borders of
China, describes the great city as it was at that time. He
writes of a thriving metropolis of wide streets, so straight
and long that a man "could see from one city gate to the
other," an unobstructed view of approximately three miles.
Merchant ships from Europe, North Africa, the Arabian
peninsula, and India crowded its wharves, justifying Benjamin's description of Alexandria as "the trading city of all
nations." The many prosperous of the population lived for

the most part in large houses facing on the avenues, and the atmosphere was as open and unrestrained as that of Fez had been claustrophobic and repressive. In addition to the world-famous Academy of Aristotle, the city and its environs was home to some twenty institutions of higher learning in which students from all segments of the populace studied a wide variety of subjects. It was a great cosmopolitan center, which from its founding by Alexander the Great in 332 B.C.E. had been the home of a large Jewish population that was an integral part of its commercial and cultural activities. Politically prominent Jews were regularly involved in the life of the ruling court of Egypt and in the circles of government in Alexandria.

The Jewish community of approximately 3,000 families made up a significant portion of the city's population of 50,000. Not only did the Jews throughout all Egypt live in religious freedom, but they enjoyed a large measure of civil autonomy, at least over their own internal affairs. Their schools, religious institutions, communal functions, and systems of justice were under the administrative hand of the government-appointed *nagid*, a national office that had existed since the tenth century. From Cairo, the *nagid* gave formal appointive office to rabbis, judges, and other officials and represented Jewish interests at the caliph's court, in addition often serving as his physician.

Only a few months after the family arrived in Alexandria, the health of Rabbi Maimon began to fail rapidly. When he died after a period of sharp decline, letters of condolence and tribute poured in from every part of the known world where Jews lived or traveled, reflecting his stature as a religious scholar. Moses was now head of the family, and decisions would have to be made about how he would provide for his brother and sister. The brothers' trading business in precious stones was enlarging, but it was hardly sufficient for the purpose. Moses was encouraged by friends to apply for a formal paid position as a rabbi, but he refused. It was anathema to him that his learning and his religious leadership and counsel should be compensated with money. He was forceful in his opinion—consistent with more than a millennium of Jewish tradition—that rabbis should under no circumstances be salaried officials. Refusing to "use the Torah as a spade," Moses wrote a pamphlet addressing the issue in which he made the point that history is replete with examples of eminent rabbis who worked at regular jobs in order to support themselves. Even the great Hillel, he pointed out, was a woodcutter, and his frequent disputant, Shammai, was a carpenter. Others were potters, weavers, smiths, sandalmakers, and the like. He told of Rabbi Karna, a water carrier who asked the community to replace his wages if he had to leave work to judge a matter of law. Rejecting the common custom in Alexandria, Moses ben Maimon would not accept money for doing the work of God.

Just how the family survived financially during this period is uncertain, but a clue may be found in the pamphlet. Moses wrote that he considered it permissible for a scholar to give money to someone else to invest, and then to share the profits with him. Very likely, he considered his business arrangements with his brother to fit into that category. It was probably about this time that the two came to the agreement that David would become the family's main source of support as their business grew, leaving his brother free to devote the greatest part of his time to scholarly studies. Henceforth, David would do all of the trading.

When Moses arrived in Alexandria in 1165 at the age of twenty-seven, the reigning Egyptian caliph was el Adid, who was destined to be the last of the Fatimid dynasty to rule the country. Within three years, Egypt would fall prey to the constant battling among a trio of contenders: Amalric, Frankish king of the Crusaders in Palestine; the Syrians under Sultan Nureddin; and the Fatimid Egyptians themselves. Alexandria would come to be occupied during the period of strife by the Syrians under the command of Saladin, the nephew of Nureddin's Kurdish vizier, Shirkuh. The people of the city abhorred the alliance that el Adid made with Amalric's Christians against the Syrians, and resentment lingered even after all foreign forces had been withdrawn. The unrest, which in fact existed throughout Egypt, was complicated by a problem that has in one or another form plagued Arab countries for centuries before that time and since: The Fatimids were Shiites, and the majority of their subjects were Sunni. Shiites reject the oral tradition of Islam, accepting only the written Koran; the Sunni, who are therefore considered the more orthodox, accept both the oral and the written law.

A problem of the same sort was causing difficulties in the Jewish community as well, due to the presence in Alexandria of a large number of Karaite families. Karaism, a movement that had its origins in eighth-century Persia (and that still exists among small groups in Israel, Poland, and parts of the former Soviet Union), was analogous to Shiism in the sense of rejecting anything but the Hebrew Bible as the source of all divine law. Because it repudiated rabbinic Judaism, it was considered heretical by the regular Jewish congregations, with the result that very little religious interchange took place between the two groups. They would not eat in each other's homes, bury each other's dead, or even acknowledge that their religious goals were similar. Because the Karaites had no designated leader, they were under the authority of the *nagid*, who was chosen from among the orthodox group. This hardly helped the situation, since successive *nagids* (in Hebrew, *negidim*) had decried the rituals of the Karaites as heretical and devoid of the inspiring thought that had entered Judaism through the rabbinic additions and interpretations.

But the Karaites had nevertheless thrived, at least in the economic and social sense. And even in the intellectual sense, there were those who found their principles more than a little compelling. The natural sympathy that existed between them and the Shiite Fatimids had been to their great advantage, not only in commerce but in public affairs as well. Many of them had become wealthy and politically influential throughout Egypt, notwithstanding their submission to the *nagid*. Their strong position in local affairs emboldened them in attempts, sometimes successful, to draw the orthodox into their camp—especially in respect to mixed marriages. The conflict between two groups so mutually scornful of each other was a danger to both of them. Though there was no way to bring the two together in matters of ritual or custom, some kind of resolution was needed that might lessen the frictions.

For all its prosperity, the Jewish community of Alexandria was not a learned one, and generally not as observant as Moses would have liked. The Jews had taken advantage of the secular opportunities available to them and become far more worldly than he thought appropriate. Their rabbis were in general less knowledgeable than elsewhere, and their religious academies were not a source of leadership. Familiarity with Torah and Talmud—and with religious scholarship in general—was not at a very high level. In such an atmosphere, Moses's considerable knowledge and wisdom in religious matters soon became apparent and his advice repeatedly sought. It was inevitable that he should have become embroiled in the orthodox community's conflict with the Karaites. His position became public through his answer to a letter from a local Jewish man asking him to comment on the situation.

Moses replied in the form called a responsum, the name given to a written reply by a rabbinical authority to questions sent from Jews anywhere in the world. These judgments carried great weight, somewhat in the manner that judicial precedents do today. The responsa of Maimonides, written over the course of decades, would become a major archive for recording his thought and the events of his life. Responsa remain to this day a valuable method of authoritative comment on problems that come up in the course of Jewish life. It is said that the Rambam wrote some six hundred of them, of which multiple copies were usually made by the recipients, for widespread distribution.

As much as Moses abhorred the practices of the Karaites and favored a complete separation from them, he continued to hold out the hope that they could be brought back to the fold of orthodoxy. Though he did not yet have the power that in later years would come to him, the letter of response advocated not only tolerance but respect for the sect. Social relationships between the groups were to be maintained and even strengthened, he said. Orthodox Jews should offer to the Karaites such rituals as circumcision and burial rites previously denied them, but at the same time he made it clear that the rival sect should be considered a corruptive influence; having violated the intentions of God, they were not, he insisted, authentic Jews. They were to be refused permission to make up the quorum of ten (called a minyan) required as an assemblage for prayer, and they should not be included among the three men needed to pray after a meal. In effect, Maimonides was excluding Karaites from participation in the most fundamental of the communal Jewish rituals: daily prayer and meals.

This was a step more radical than any leader of the

Alexandrian Jewish community had yet dared take, and it did not sit well with the socially and politically powerful Karaites. Even some in the orthodox group took exception to what they considered the harshness of Moses's decision and the presumptuousness of such a young man in making it. Facing this degree of opposition, Moses had to decide whether remaining in Alexandria was worth the conflict that was sure to ensue. From the time of his arrival, he had been uncomfortable in this milieu, where the level of Jewish learning and observance was inadequate. The decision was not difficult: Instead of railing against his opposition, Moses did quite the opposite. Barely two years after arriving, he decided to emigrate once more.

The time seemed propitious. Moses was nearing the completion of his great work, *Kitab al-Siraj* (*Perush al ha-Mishnah*, or *Commentary on the Mishnah*), after ten years of concentrated effort. During the course of its writing, the *Commentary* had become far more than an explication of Jewish law and an extraction of the basic halakha from the myriad tendrils of Talmudic discussion in which it had become entwined. Its author had chosen to use its composition as an opportunity to present his philosophy of Judaism and to expound on concepts that he believed to have long been misinterpreted, not only by ordinary people but by some of the rabbinical authorities themselves. In doing this, he focused as much on moral and social responsibilities as he did on observance and ritual. The final text was infused with principles that we would now recognize as psychology and ethics. He did not hesitate to make use of his wide knowledge of Greek philosophy and its methods of reasoning, and also of what was then known of the findings of science. And he had remained true to his original intent of accessibility to persons of every educational background, provided only that they could speak Arabic. In accomplishing his aim of popularizing the Mishnah, he produced a text that could guide the life of any Arabic-speaking Jew—and all others, too, once translations into Hebrew had been done—living in any place during those difficult years of the twelfth century.

With this in mind, Maimonides began every one of the six sections of the *Commentary* with an introduction, in which he provided not only a dissertation on the structure of that portion of Oral Law, but the historical background of how it came to be, from Mount Sinai to the completion of Judah ha-Nasi's Mishnah. Because he did not always agree with the teachings of the Gemara and later rabbinic commentators, he did not hesitate to ignore them or to point out where he thought they were wrong in their judgments, but always with an eye to avoid entering into the complexities of their reasoning or the tortuous pathways by which they reached conclusions. The result is that, taken as a whole, the six sections of the *Commentary* provided a new and unique perspective on Judaism, originating in the mind of the only authority of that time who had an intellectual background sufficiently eclectic to produce it. Had Maimonides written nothing else, this first great work would have justified the slogan still heard today, "From Moses [of the Bible] to Moses [Maimonides], there arose no one like Moses."

An example of this kind of eclectic originality was the Rambam's musings on the soul. Not only the body, he wrote, is capable of being healthy or sick, but also the soul, which may turn toward evil and wrong ways of thinking. He was convinced that such deviations from health are not inborn, but are acquired from outside influences; they become ingrained with long practice. Just as one would consult a physician to treat a disease of the body, a sage or teacher should be consulted to cure a sick soul. Even if a man develops a predilection for a particular vice, he can overcome it by the determination to do otherwise.

Thus, there is choice in whether to continue in the paths of wickedness or to pursue a life of morality. But, argued Maimonides, there is such a thing as trying to be overly good, which leads to excesses of its own, like self-deprivation, rigidity, and overweening pride. To Maimonides, turning to either extreme is spiritual illness.

> Inordinate passion—the extreme of excess—and total insensibility to enjoyment—the extreme of deficiency—are both absolutely pernicious. The psychic dispositions from which these two extremes result—the one being an exaggeration and the other a deficiency—are alike classified among moral imperfections.

Likewise, liberality is the Mean between sordidness and extravagance; courage, between recklessness and cowardice; dignity, between haughtiness and loutishness; humility, between arrogance and self-abasement; contentedness, between avarice and slothful indifference; and munificence, between meanness and profusion; modesty, between impudence and shamefacedness. So it is with other qualities. . . . The really praiseworthy is the medium course of action to which everyone should strive to adhere, always weighing his conduct carefully, so that he may attain the proper Mean.

Here Maimonides is invoking the Greek ideal of the golden mean as a way, for example, to avoid immorality on the one hand and asceticism or self-righteousness on the other. Stating a premise that would be echoed in later writings, he pointed out that the ascetic life weakens and destroys the body, which must remain healthy if the highest purpose of the soul—to acquire wisdom and the knowledge of God—is to be realized. And all of this depends on the fact that man has free will.

Were not man master of his own life, it would be useless, in fact, absolutely in vain, for man to study, to instruct, for a man to learn an art, as it would be entirely impossible for him, on account of the external force compelling him . . . to gain certain knowledge, or to acquire a certain characteristic. Reward and punishment, too, would be pure injustice, both as regards man toward man, and as between God and man. . . . This theory [that all is preordained] is, therefore, positively unsound, contrary to reason and common sense, subversive of the fundamental principles of religion, and attributes injustice to God (far be it from Him). In reality, the undoubted truth of the matter is that man has full sway over all his actions. If he wishes to do a thing, he does it; if he does not wish to do it, he need not, for there is no external compulsion controlling him. There God very properly commanded man, saying, "See, I have set before thee this day life and the good, death and evil . . . therefore choose life."

In stating his opposition to any notion of predestination, Maimonides included his repudiation of every influence in such matters beyond man's own decisions. Belief in astrology, for example, was rampant in those times even among Jews, and the *Commentary* condemned it in the most severe terms. In another part of the text, the practice of inscribing the name of God in amulets is subjected to scorn, as a superstition unworthy of a rational man.

Also condemned are fanciful conceptions of what the afterlife would be like. *Olam ha-Ba*, the world to come, had traditionally been believed to be either a place of sensual pleasures, infinite bounty of food, drink, clothing, and riches; the satisfaction of every whim including physical beauty; reunion with family and friends; or all of these things combined with punishment of those who have been wicked, for whom a special place of pain is reserved. Maimonides scoffed at such notions, describing them as the beliefs of foolish or ignorant people who did not understand the metaphors by which sages had traditionally described the world to come and the advent of the Messiah. Such descriptions were not to be taken literally, he taught. They were only meant to appeal to naive minds, in order to draw them toward belief, in the same way that one offers candy and toys to children as a way of inducing them to their studies because they are not yet ready to comprehend abstract notions or to value study for its own sake. The afterlife, Moses asserted, should not be thought of in terms of reward and punishment; the resurrection of the body was not assured for all. He did not subscribe to the Mishnah's promise that "all Israelites have a share in *Olam ha-Ba.*" In the scheme of Maimonides, only the righteous would be resurrected, though he did not specify in what form. The resurrection was to be thought of more in intellectual terms than in physical ones: The immortal being enjoys the bliss of contemplating God, to which no other pleasure can be compared. In essence, he was describing an *Olam ha-Ba* of intellectual enlightenment, achieved through a heightened state of spiritual communion with God. This is a form of afterlife that man, who thinks of pleasure as deriving from his senses, cannot comprehend as long as he is alive. As for punishment of the wicked, it will consist of the destruction of their souls, in order that they may not achieve what is granted to the righteous. Rather than punishment by some form of torture, their destiny is nonexistence.

The Messiah, too, wrote Maimonides, will not be what is popularly thought. He will be like a mortal man but far wiser, and he will restore the house of David from which he springs and then lead the Jews toward the political independence in Palestine that will allow their studious application to the principles of Torah—for, to the Rambam, the notion of a messianic time was ultimately a political concept. Other than that, the world will remain substantially the same after the Messiah's coming, minus its hardships. The necessities of life will be more easily available in order to free men to study. In time, the Messiah will die as men do, to be succeeded by descendants who will maintain his heritage and continue his Davidic line. To Maimonides, the coming of the Messiah did not have supernatural implications of the sort long anticipated.

It might be thought that Maimonides, having expressed while in Fez the liberal viewpoint that pseudo-conversion and dissembling to save one's life are permissible, would be equally liberal in defining the standards for a believing Jew. But quite the opposite position is taken in the *Commentary*. In fact, such strict standards are laid down in the text that they have been the cause for controversy ever since. Neither in the Bible nor in any rabbinic writings had there previously been any hint of dogma so firmly stated that to reject them was to be rejected in turn from the possibility of achieving *Olam ha-Ba*—and suddenly there they were, in the form of the Thirteen Principles of the Faith, dictates from a thirty-year-old who was increasingly being recognized as an authoritative voice in the community of Egyptian Jews. To Maimonides, violation of so much as a single one of these principles meant violation of the contract with Judaism. They are as follows:

1. I believe with perfect faith that the Creator, blessed be his name, is the Author and Guide of everything that has been created, and that he alone has made, does make, and will make all things.

2. I believe with perfect faith that the Creator, blessed be his name, is a unity, and that there is no unity in any manner like unto his, and that he alone is our God, who was, is, and will be.

3. I believe with perfect faith that the Creator, blessed be his name, is not a body, and that he is free from all accidents of matter, and that he has not any form whatsoever.

4. I believe with perfect faith that the Creator, blessed be his name, is the first and the last.

5. I believe with perfect faith that to the Creator, blessed be his name, and to him alone, it is right to pray, and that it is not right to pray to any being besides him.

6. I believe with perfect faith that all the words of the prophets are true.

7. I believe with perfect faith that the prophecy of Moses our teacher, peace be unto him, was true, and that he was the chief of our prophets, both of those that preceded him and of those that followed him.

8. I believe with perfect faith that the whole law, now in our possession, is the same that was given to Moses our teacher, peace be unto him.

9. I believe with perfect faith that this law will not be changed, and that there will never be any other law from the Creator, blessed be his name.

10. I believe with perfect faith that the Creator, blessed be his name, knows every deed of the children of men, and all their thoughts, as it is said. It is he that fashioneth the hearts of them all, that giveth heed to all their deeds.

11. I believe with perfect faith that the Creator, blessed be his name, rewards those that keep his commandments, and punishes those that transgress them.

12. I believe with perfect faith in the coming of the Messiah, and, though he tarry, I will wait daily for his coming.

13. I believe with perfect faith that there will be a resurrection of the dead at the time when it shall please the Creator, blessed be his name, and exalted be the remembrance of him for ever and ever.

The thirteenth principle would seem to be at odds with Maimonides' contention that resurrection should not be thought of in terms of the physical body. But the issue of what is, in fact, resurrected is here left somewhat ambiguous, very likely on purpose.

It was in his *Commentary on the Mishnah* that Moses first articulated a theme that would frequently recur throughout his writings, whether in the books or his many letters, namely that the words of Torah and Talmud are not always to be taken literally. Much of the holy writings, he said, are in the form of metaphor, with the deeper meaning only to be understood by those with the proper training and intellect. The purpose of this literary device, he pointed out, was to attract to the Law those with simpler minds and education, for otherwise the profundity of the text would turn them away from it. But the underlying motive was to ensure that "the mind of the student might be sharpened, and so that these matters might remain a secret from those whose intellect is inadequate to receive truth in its purity." With this in mind, he advocated that the principles of reward for good deeds and punishment for evil were to be taught to ordinary people, although a learned man knows that the real reason to do good is for its own sake, virtue being its own reward. "The reward of a good deed is the good deed, and the punishment for sin is sin."

It is obvious from all of the foregoing that the *Commentary on the Mishnah* was a highly personal work, as was everything that ever came from the pen of Maimonides. He concluded it with a reflection on the hardships he had endured during the ten long years of its composition. He had been forced to travel from place to place, he noted, sometimes studying and writing on shipboard, "my heart afflicted by the miseries of the time, by the fate of exile that God has brought upon us, by the constant expulsions and wanderings from one end of the world to the other. But perhaps this is a grace, for exile atones for sin. . . . God knows that I have explained some chapters while on my wanderings, and others on board ships, in inns, on roadsides and without any access to books. Besides, I have devoted myself to the study of the sciences."

Other of the *Commentary*'s concluding sentences reveal two seemingly disparate aspects of the personality of the thirty-year-old scholar who was writing them. On the one hand, he writes with humility of the difficulties of the work, as though to explain the long time it took to complete it and the probability that some readers will find passages worthy of disagreement. He asks for criticism and goes so far as to defend those who will provide it, against the resentment of men who might be offended by their comments: "Criticism is not an act of injustice; it is rewarded by heaven. It is dear to me, for it is a divine craft."

But another paragraph of conclusion has a very different tone. This young teacher, whose stated intent was to clarify the abstruse nature of Jewish law so that it could be comprehended by anyone willing to study his text, now looks down from a magisterial height to admonish his readers that they are engaged in a project that can be accomplished only by intense and repeated application to his text. Implicit in the following paragraph is a declaration of authority, as though the work were so definitive that those who disagree with it must be doing so only because they have not yet mastered its contents or appreciated its truths.

> Read my book over and over and reflect on it carefully. If your vanity should mislead you to believe that you understand the contents after one reading or even ten, then, by God, you have been misled to foolishness. You must not advance hastily in the perusal of this book. For I have not just written it down haphazardly, but only after long research and reflection.

It is difficult to evaluate the significance of this passage, reflecting as it does a certain intellectual self-regard that a modern reader might well be justified in decrying. But in weighing these sentences against what is known of their author's character and the circumstances in which he was writing, reasons for their somewhat imperious tone easily suggest themselves. Those reasons, in fact, might explain other aspects of the *Commentary* that would seem contradictory to the image of forbearance, liberality, and empathy that characterized so much of the writing and judgments of Maimonides.

Expulsions, forced conversion, individual murders, and the wholesale slaughter of entire ghettoized communities were decimating the population of Jews living in the Christian countries. The harsh rule of the Almohads in Spain and

North Africa threatened the future of Jewish life in the territories they controlled. Only in Egypt was there any measure of real freedom, and even here dangers lurked, although of a very different kind. For while Jews prospered and practiced their religion unhindered, that very freedom had led to a laxity in observance and an erosion of scholarship and of the regard paid to rabbinical teachings and the Law itself. Not only was the spiritual life of the Jews in danger, but their disappearance into a sea of assimilation and conversion was more than a remote possibility. In addition to everything else, there were the Karaites, a heretical sect seeking converts from their orthodox brethren, a temptation to which more than a few succumbed, largely because of the affluence and political power of the heretics. There was real danger that the Jewish people would disappear.

To Maimonides, the only solution to the looming threat to Jewish survival was the spiritual equivalent of circling the wagons. This was not an abstract theoretical notion but a matter of utmost necessity, with immediate practical importance. It was imperative that the Jews have strong leadership and well-defined rules by which to live their daily lives, or before long there would be no Jews. The remoteness in both era and atmosphere of the Mishnah meant that a contemporary text was needed; the abstruse nature of the Gemara meant that a path through its thickets was needed; the current tendency for spiritual drift meant that well-defined rules of behavior and thought were needed. To all of this, Maimonides responded with his *Commentary on the Mishnah*.

It laid out his conception of what had to be done if the Jews were to be saved from their enemies and from their own disregard of proper observance and study. In even small deviations he saw the beginnings of the problems to which he had been witness in every territory where his cheerless wanderings had taken him. There could be no compromise. The *Commentary on the Mishnah* was more than just a text meant to guide his people back to the path that would save them from extinction: It was his assertion of leadership, his declaration that in his teachings the way was being shown.

The *Commentary* did not achieve its author's objective. As great as was Maimonides' accomplishment, its message hardly met with universal acceptance. Objections were soon raised to various of its themes, and some can be heard to this day. Not surprisingly, the unforgiving nature of the Thirteen Principles of the Faith was anathema to many Jews, especially the precept that *Olam ha-Ba* was to be denied should a single one be violated. The notion of any credo at all, in fact, seemed to some to be a concept closer to Christianity or Islam than to Judaism, in which an entire Torah was the basis of faith.

To some readers, the very act of intertwining the author's own viewpoints and his occasional disagreements with Talmudic judgments was a presumptuous thing to do, especially for a young man who had not yet achieved a position of authority beyond areas where he was known personally. The interjection of certain elements of a scientific nature and the consideration of Greek philosophy did not sit well with those who felt that such matters should be kept separate from religious thought. Some were bothered by the *Commentary*'s idiosyncratic mix of progressive thought and rigid faith.

The *Commentary*'s cause was not helped by its having been written in Arabic, but Maimonides had little choice if he was to reach the ordinary man whose ability to understand Hebrew was deficient. Although fluency in the Hebrew language was far from universal, almost everyone could read the letters. By using them to write in Arabic, Jewish authors of the time assured themselves of an orthographic barrier, making it unlikely that Muslims would take the trouble to attempt penetration of their text. But this meant that only readers in the Arab lands had access to the *Commentary*. Until the book was translated into the ancient tongue by Samuel ibn Tibbon in 1202, almost forty years after its first appearance, it could not be read by Jews in the Christian countries.

Adding to the problems standing in the way of wide acceptance—even after ibn Tibbon's translation—was the fact that Rashi, a native of the French city of Troyes, had written his well-received commentary on the Talmud about a hundred years earlier, and it had been incorporated into the text. The Franco-German Jews were not about to displace the work of their greatest luminary.

For these reasons, the Maimonidean *Commentary on the Mishnah* did not have the effect its author had hoped for. Although certain of its controversial aspects became the object of discussion in interested quarters, the book did not otherwise cause much of a stir. It seemed to change nothing in the world of Arabic-speaking Jews, and it added little to its author's reputation, except to increase the respect in which he was already held in strictly scholarly circles. Even though he was sufficiently known by this time that he was receiving many requests for opinions on matters of faith, his prominence was not sufficient, for example, for him to be mentioned in the writings of Benjamin of Tudela, who visited Cairo shortly after the *Commentary*'s publication in 1168 and was making a point of meeting all well-known Jews. By then, Moses had left Alexandria and taken up residence in Fustat, a city near the Egyptian capital. It was there that his greatest work would be done.

# Tragedy and Depression

Fustat, a city already more than five hundred years old when Maimonides settled there in 1168, had been the capital of Egypt until nearby Cairo superseded it when the Fatimids seized control of the country in 969 and began their dynasty. It was a thriving, prosperous center of commerce and banking, noted for its glassware and ceramics industries. The Jews had done well there, living on peaceful, even friendly terms with their Muslim neighbors and generally belonging to the economic group we would today call middle class. Being the traditional home of the *nagid*, it was the center from which the Jewish community of Egypt found its religious and administrative bearings.

The affluent inhabitants of Fustat tended to live in areas that consisted primarily of homes, without nearby commercial buildings. But aside from those relatively small neighborhoods, the city had grown rather haphazardly through the centuries, with such little planning that residential and commercial zones were intermixed in large parts of it, where people of various socioeconomic strata lived alongside one another, often adjacent to shops and more substantial places of business. The result was that mercantile structures and groups of run-down and neglected homes that were little more than shacks stood side by side with well-kept houses where families of some means dwelt in comfort or even luxury. Although the Jews lived freely among Muslims, they did congregate around synagogues, so that, as has always happened, they predominated in certain neighborhoods.

Jewish families lived very much as the Muslims did: They wore similar clothing and bought their goods in the same shops. Aside from differences imposed by the dietary restrictions of each group, they ate the same foods as their gentile neighbors. The turbaned and loosely gowned men would have been indistinguishable from any of their Arab fellows but for the large, fringed prayer shawl that was worn wrapped around the upper part of the body at all times. There was an air of homogeneity about the society, though a deeper look would have revealed that the Jews lived in very much the same second-class status as they had in Cordoba even during the best years of tolerance.

While in Alexandria, Maimonides would have had plenty of contact with the Jewish community of Fustat, and would have corresponded with men who helped him find a suitable home for his family before he arrived. With the gem business growing as it was, the Maimons would have moved into a large house where they lived in comfort, in an area close to a synagogue among whose congregants were several serious scholars. Fustat provided the proper atmosphere in which to put the final touches to the *Commentary on the Mishnah*.

But shortly after the book was completed, a political and military upheaval overtook what had until then been a peaceful city. Following a battlefield defeat in 1160, the Fatimids had agreed to pay tribute to the Christian king of Jerusalem, but el Adid never fulfilled the obligation. In October 1168, the Christians under Amalric invaded Egypt and marched without much opposition northward toward Cairo, pillaging cities and murdering large numbers of people along the way. The capital was so well fortified that it could resist capture, but Fustat was entirely without defenses, and Amalric was determined to take it. El Adid's vizier ordered the inhabitants of the city to take whatever possessions they could and leave immediately for Cairo, after which he sent in slaves carrying some twenty thousand bottles of petroleum, which they ignited in an attempt to burn everything to the ground.

Abetted by the large number of ramshackle houses scattered in clusters throughout all but a few precincts, a raging inferno engulfed the city. Set on November 22, 1168, the flames, constantly reigniting collections of rubble, did not fully subside until the middle of January the following year. But the frustrated Amalric would not be denied. When the Christian king laid siege to Cairo, el Adid sent word to Nureddin, the sultan of Syria, begging him for help. It is said that his emissary to Damascus carried with him hair from the heads of el Adid's wives, as a special plea warning of what would happen to the Muslim women should they fall into the hands of the Christian king's marauding troops. Nureddin sent an army under the command of his vizier, Shirkuh, upon whose approach Amalric retreated in haste.

Not unexpectedly, the Egyptian vizier, Shawar, grumbled at the power newly invested in Nureddin's general and his young nephew, Saladin. Before long, he began plotting to regain his authority. When Saladin caught wind of the plans, he demanded that steps be taken to end the threat, including the execution of Shawar. To placate him, the weak-willed caliph had his vizier beheaded and replaced by Shirkuh, to whom he presented the head as a token of cooperation with the saviors of his capital. Shirkuh ruled only until March 1169, when he unexpectedly died. Saladin took over as vizier, gradually increasing his power and restoring the majority's Sunni rituals to a country long under the Shiite dominance of the Fatimids. This move ensured him the allegiance of the suppressed group, especially because he himself was a Sunnite. By 1171 he was easily able to depose the ineffectual el Adid, whose overthrow was facilitated by the onset of an illness that would take his life later that year. With the ascendancy of Saladin, the fortunes of Egypt were set off on a new and illustrious course.

Among Saladin's first projects was the rebuilding of Fustat. As so often happens when a city is restored after its destruction, an economic boom took place. Confident in the administration of the popular Saladin, the inhabitants returned and erected new homes and commercial establishments. The city was soon thriving. It was the ideal time for new beginnings, in which Maimonides would share.

Shortly after his arrival in Fustat, Moses had begun to take an interest in the religious affairs of the 7,000 Jewish families who lived there and in Cairo, which was less than two miles away (so close that Fustat is a section of today's Cairo). He was particularly concerned that the descendants of the Babylonian Jews living in the area followed certain practices that were materially different from those to which the Jews of Palestinian origin adhered. The most important of these had to do with such matters as the order of the prayer service and whether the cycle of time for the reading of the entire Torah should be one year or three. He attempted to adjudicate, but found himself up against divisions so entrenched that the two groups prayed in different synagogues. That his efforts were largely in vain is hardly surprising considering the enduring history of such controversies.

Another of Moses's concerns was the status of the many Jews who had been taken captive and enslaved in the wars of the period, originally by the Crusaders and later by the forces of the Christian Kingdom of Jerusalem, and even by some Muslim chieftains. In addition to these were the smaller number who had been taken on the high seas by pirates or the ships of various rulers, and were either in slave captivity or being held for ransom. In the campaign to free them, he was more successful than he had been in his frustrating attempt to reunite the disparate factions among his people. By personal appeal, by the formation of committees, and by letter, he was able to raise enough money from Jews in Arab and some Christian communities to ransom many of the captives.

Activities like these helped to make Moses well known, and to raise his stature among the many who heard about them. Very likely, he was able to be so effective in raising the funds because he was already becoming prominent for his learning and judgment, but such ventures certainly increased his recognition among Jews, Christians, and Arabs alike. It is of some significance in this regard that a marriage certificate of 1171 bears his signature and the following statement: "With the permission of our lord Moses, the Grand Rabbi in Israel." The title of grand rabbi seems to have been an honorary one, because there is no official documentation of his having been formally declared to hold such an office. Still, the Muslim authorities were by this time referring to him as *ra'is al-Yahud*, the head of the Jews. During this period, the number of religious inquiries that were reaching him from local and distant rabbinical sources continued to grow.

While this was going on, a letter reached Moses from a leader of the world's second oldest Jewish community (Jerusalem's being the oldest), that of Yemen, asking his advice at a time when its existence was imperiled. That the Yemenites should have turned to him is a measure of the recognition he was attaining in parts of the Arab world. His response, which was widely circulated, would make him even more prominent.

The Sunni ascendancy decreed by Saladin in Egypt had created a wave of reaction in Yemen, which was a Shiite homeland. The Shiites seized power around 1172 and immediately imposed harsh restrictions that abruptly took away the freedom that Jews had long enjoyed in that remote land on the southern strip of the Arabian peninsula. Far less tolerant of other faiths than the Sunnis, they considered Christians and Jews to be infidels, unclean, and not deserving of life among the true believers. As the Almohads had done in the south of Spain and in North Africa, they began a persecution that demanded conversion or death.

Many Jews did convert, and not only because of the terror. As in other places at the time, the general level of religious learning was not high in Yemen, and apostasy had long been a danger to the integrity of the community. There was a general feeling among the less well educated that Muhammad had indeed brought a new religion to replace their own, and it must not be resisted. The rate of conversion was accelerated when the repression began, especially when those considering it saw the privations being endured by their coreligionists. Worsening the situation were the activities of several breakaway members of the Jewish community who had taken it upon themselves to go about proselytizing for Islam. Using biblical quotations, astrological

confluences, and predictions based on numerologic manipu-
lations of portentous words in scripture, they attempted to
convince the large audiences they attracted that the victory
of Islam was foretold and inevitable.

Were this not menacing enough, there arose among the
Yemenite Jews a self-anointed young prophet who claimed
that he was the herald for the coming Messiah. He had
brought dead people to life, he boasted, and would do it
again. Families were to give all their money and property to
the poor, he harangued his ever-increasing throngs of hear-
ers, in preparation for the Deliverance that was imminent.
More than once in their long history, Jews had suffered
severe punishments from a ruler because a man in their
midst had announced that he was the Messiah or his fore-
runner. In the already perilous circumstances in which they
were living, the community leaders viewed the activities of
this "prophet" with mounting alarm, and yet they were
hesitant to intervene because so many believed in his predictions, including some of their own number.

Matters became rapidly worse, and the leaders of the
community were soon in despair. A visiting merchant named
Solomon ha-Kohen, who was a great admirer of Maimonides,
urged one of them, Jacob al-Fayumi, to write to Fustat for
counsel, especially because al-Fayumi was himself uncertain
of just which path to take, being not only a believer in
astrology but having become convinced that the young man,
whether or not deluded, was sincere in his preachings.

The letter that Maimonides wrote in reply, which became

known as the *Iggeret Teman* (Letter to Yemen), or alternately as *Petah Tikvah* (Gate of Hope), was read widely in that country and later circulated throughout the Jewish communities of the Muslim world, and, probably in Hebrew translation from the original Arabic, much of the Christian world as well. Though addressed to the Yemenites, it was a message of hope to all who were living in torment under the oppressions common in almost every land. It was in many ways a statement of its author's commitment to his faith and the meaning that he found in his people's suffering.

Moses reassured the people of Yemen that the Jewish nation would always survive every attempt to annihilate it, as it had in the past. Neither the brutality of powerful monarchs nor the blandishments of religions claiming to supersede it would destroy the permanence promised by God. There were plenty of examples of tyrants who had failed in the attempt.

Be assured, my brethren, that our three opponents, namely, the system of coercion, that of sophistry, and that which seeks to impress a high origin to which it is not entitled, will vanish. They may continue to prosper for a certain time, but their glory will shortly disappear.

Our brethren of the House of Israel, scattered to the remote regions of the globe, it is your duty to strengthen one another, the older the younger, the few the many. . . . My brethren, it behooves us to keep ever present before our minds the great day of Sinai, for the Lord has forbidden us ever to forget it. Rear your offspring in a thorough understanding of that all-important event. Explain before large assemblies the principles it involves. Show that it is a lucid mirror reflecting the truth, aye, the very pivot on which our religion turns. . . . Know, moreover, you who are born in this covenant and reared in this belief, that the stupendous occurrence . . . stands alone in the annals of mankind. For a whole people heard the word of God, and saw the glory of Divinity. From this lasting memory we must draw our power to strengthen our faith even in times of persecution.

Maimonides scoffed at the claims of Muslims and Christians that their religions had replaced Judaism. He ridiculed the notion that astrology has any validity, pointing out that the science of astronomy had refuted it: "Purge your thoughts of astrology, the way one cleanses a sullied garment of filth. . . . Pay no heed when someone speaks of a superior or inferior conjunction of stars," reiterating the truth of man's free will, independent of stellar determinants. He derided those who read hidden messages in the words of the Bible, and stated his certainty that the emissary of the Messiah was more madman than fraud but in any event to be denounced. He should be put away, counseled Moses, and the Muslims advised of his disposition. "In that manner the people will be saved from persecution and peace, and harmony will be restored to the community." He reminded al-Fayumi of the persecutions that had resulted in the past when rulers had felt threatened by the rising up of false messiahs among the Jews, and had responded to the perceived danger with violence directed toward those from whose midst he had sprung.

Maimonides ridiculed the young man for predicting the imminent coming of the Messiah, pointing out that "the precise date of the messianic advent cannot be known," but he apparently did not feel that this admonition was sufficiently strong. Seemingly contradicting his own words, he then went on to tell of a tradition in his family that prophecy would return to Israel in the year 4976 (1216), to indicate that the Messiah was on his way. It is difficult to explain the inconsistency, except that 4976 was a date so far in the future that it annulled any possibility that the "prophet" was to be believed. And Moses may also have wished to reassure the Yemenite Jews that the day of messianic deliverance would one day come and was even somewhat near at hand, perhaps within the lifetimes of some of them and certainly of their children. And, of course, there is the possibility that the family tradition was real and he believed in it, though the predicted date was well beyond his own life span of the biblical three score and ten (yet within the range promised to the strong who were able to put up with the accompanying "labor and sorrow" of the added decade, as described in Psalm 90). No matter his reasons, these statements proved to be precisely what was needed at that difficult time. Maimonides might well have convinced himself that the desperate situation demanded desperate measures, and if a bit of dissembling was necessary, then he would do it.

At the end of the letter, Maimonides asked that al-Fayumi have copies made and distributed to all the scattered Jewish communities of Yemen, "in order to strengthen the people in their faith and put them on their feet. Read it in public gatherings and in private, and you will thus become a public benefactor." But he warned his correspondent not to let any gentile know the letter's contents, lest severe retribution follow and conditions only worsen. His instructions were followed; his counsel was accepted and people took heart. Renewed in their faith that the ancient bond between Israel and God would be maintained and strengthened, the Yemenites were able to overcome much of their fear and travail. Thus strengthened in their resolve, they proved willing to wait patiently for the promise of Maimonides to come true, that their oppressors would soon be vanquished.

And that is precisely what happened. In 1174, barely a year later, Saladin's brother Turhan Shah entered Yemen and took control of its government, thus liberating the Jews from their difficulties and providing the same kind of freedom that existed in Egypt. Maimonides, already greatly admired for his spiritual rescue of the despairing community, now became a man revered throughout Yemen. A special prayer for his welfare was inserted into the regular service each day. It asked that God establish His kingdom on earth "during the life of all the house of Israel and during the life of Moses, the son of Maimon." As word of his beneficence reached other parts of the Jewish world, the reputation of Moses was further enhanced. He was seen not only as a comforter of the distressed, but as a sage who had incorporated the most significant principles of Judaism into the letter in such a way that every person who heard them—from the simplest to the wisest—was uplifted and renewed. He was the leader to whom Jews everywhere could turn for guidance and authority.

As for the false prophet, within a few months of the public readings of *Petah Tikvah*, he was arrested and brought in chains before the Shiite ruler of Yemen, who demanded proof that he had been sent by God. The deranged young man asked that his head be cut off, in order to demonstrate that it would immediately replant itself on the stump of his neck. The ruler obliged, and thus ended the story of the Messiah's herald.

No matter its circuitous nature and attendant hardships, the life of Moses Maimonides had until this time pursued an unyielding course toward a life of study, the writing of books, and leadership of the worldwide Jewish community. The mundane concerns of getting and spending had never been more than a small part of his responsibility, even in the recent years during which the family gem business was flourishing. David saw to it that the mind of his older brother was never beset by worldly cares that might divert a probing intellect from its chosen path. Though the world did keep intruding with its afflictions and sorrows, Moses was able to face them with the same combination of logical thought and religious faith that he applied to study.

Neither Moses nor David ever questioned the way in which their pact had come to be, because it was a natural outgrowth of their relationship. David, nine years younger than Moses, had been not only the cherished younger brother, but the pupil as well. Virtually all of David's wide knowledge of Jewish law and custom was learned at the side of his devoted teacher, Moses. They had sustained and brightened each other's lives during the worst of their family's ordeals after leaving Cordoba.

As the business grew, it became necessary for David to do ever more traveling. At first this involved joining mercantile caravans that went from place to place in North Africa and then Egypt, but in time it was required that he make sea voyages of varying duration. It was bad enough that his loved ones had to worry about the ever present danger of marauding desert tribes during the overland trips, but the seafaring added concerns about pirates and shipwrecks. Moses would pray for his brother's safety at these times, and he remained restless until seeing David's face again. Before every such adventure—for they were indeed hazardous undertakings—Moses would compose a letter, essentially a prayer for his safe return, and send it to David at the place of embarkation.

A copy of such a letter has been found, written to David as he prepared for a particularly auspicious journey to India in 1174. This was to be a gem-trading venture that promised to bring huge profits to the family and to others who had entrusted their precious stones to the daring merchant. The letter read in part:

> The Lord alone knows the anguish and dreariness in
>     my heart
> When parting from my beloved brother and friend.
> May the Lord guard him from harm, and reunite me
>     with him in Egypt, if the Lord so wills.

It was not to be. The ship went down in the Indian Ocean, and all aboard were drowned. Lost with the beloved David were all the precious stones except the few that had been left at home. From a level of affluence they had not enjoyed since their days in Cordoba, the remaining Maimon family was reduced to near poverty.

Still not fully recovered from his father's death, Moses was devastated by the loss of David. Neither his faith nor his philosophy was able to help him as he sank deeper and deeper into the grip of a depression so profound that he could barely function. Years later, he would write a letter to Japhet ben Iliahu, the *dayyan* of Acre, who had become his friend during his brief time in the Holy Land, in which he described his grief:

> In Egypt . . . the most terrible blow which befell me,
> a blow which caused me more grief than anything I
> have experienced in my life, was the death of the most

perfect and righteous man, who was drowned while traveling in the Indian Ocean, and with him was lost considerable money belonging to me, himself and others. He left me his widow and a little daughter to take care of.

For nearly a year after I received the sad news, I lay on my bed struggling with fever and despair. Eight years have since passed, and I still mourn, for there is no consolation. What can console me? He grew up on my knees; he was my brother, my pupil. He was engaged in business and earned money that I might stay at home and continue my studies. He was learned in the Talmud and in the Bible and an accomplished grammarian. My one joy was to see him. Now my joy has been changed into darkness. He has gone to his eternal home, and has left me prostrated in a strange land. Whenever I come across his handwriting or one of his books, my heart grows faint within me and my grief reawakens. In short: "I will go down into the grave unto my son mourning." Were not the study of the Torah my delight, and did not the study of philosophy divert me from grief, I should have succumbed in my affliction.

When this letter was written, enough years had passed so that Moses was indeed once again deeply immersed in the Torah and in philosophy, but it had taken a long time before he was able to reach that stage. The refuge he sought in study and writing had eluded him for at least a year following David's death. Inconsolable and unable to bear the sights and sounds around him, he escaped, as severely depressed people often do, to his bed. He remained in that state for a year, during which he was afflicted not only with the burden of his depression but also with fevers and problems he ascribed to his heart, though there is no record of what they were. He tells of a rash, but it would be folly to speculate about a psychosomatic origin.

Much later, when he had been practicing medicine for some years, Maimonides would write a treatise describing depression, whose reader can only think that he was telling of his own:

> When a man with a powerful frame, a sonorous voice and a radiant complexion hears sudden news that greatly afflicts him, one can see his face turning pale, the glow dimming, the body hunching, the voice faltering, and when he tries with all his might to raise his voice, he is unable to do so. For his strength is so weakened. Indeed, he often trembles with feebleness, his pulse slows down, his eyes move back in their sockets. His eyelids grow so heavy that he cannot move them, his body becomes cold and his appetite vanishes.

As the worst of the depression began to clear, Moses looked around him and saw the reality of what must be done. The few gems David had left behind had been sold, and only a little money remained. He was a thirty-six-year-old man without resources, responsible for a household consisting of David's wife, her sister and young daughter, his own sister, a freed slave, and several servants. Though the record is uncertain, he had probably married by then or would soon do so. How could he earn a living?

To be paid for teaching the Torah was anathema to him. This was a principle he had reiterated over and over, and he would not abandon it regardless of the dire circumstances in which he now found himself. But he was a man widely educated in philosophy and in the science of the time. Philosophy, in fact, was in its own way almost as precious to him as the study of the Law. And now it might help him overcome some of his financial problems, if he could lecture and teach in the subject. But an income derived solely in this way would not come close to providing for the needs of Moses's large household. He therefore turned to thoughts of practicing medicine.

Since his childhood days of poring over Maimon's copies of medical texts, Moses had been fascinated by the processes of disease and the ways in which the body yields to illness and then attempts to rally against it. He had read widely in the volumes attributed to the two Greek masters, Hippocrates and Galen, and was familiar with the works of those who followed them, such as Aretaeus, Soranus, Paul of Aegina, and Oribasius. He had learned of medicinal plants from the great herbal written by the medical botanist Dioscorides in the first century C.E., and of course he knew the biological theories of Aristotle as though he had done the experiments and made the observations himself.

It is hardly necessary to add that Moses, being the thorough scholar that he was, would also have studied the more recent treatises of the leading physicians who wrote in Arabic, including his tenth-century rabbinic predecessor, Isaac Judaeus. Three of them who were Muslims—Albucasis, Avenzoar, and the man who may have been his old friend, Averroës—had, in fact, been born in or near Cordoba. The greatest of the Muslim physicians, however, came from Persia, and Moses was certainly assiduous in learning from the volumes of clinical medicine they had produced. These were Rhazes, Haly Abbas, and Avicenna. Though the first two had been dead for two hundred years and the third for a century, their theories and practical advice dominated not only the Islamic world but the Christian world as well. It was a time when the Europeans did not produce many medical men of note, and monarchs throughout the known world sought out Arabs and Jews to be their personal physicians, even in the many lands where there were few Muslims and persecutions of the Jewish population were rampant.

Moses must have realized that his medical education— though he had acquired it not from practical bedside training but from books and from years of discussions with physicians who were his or Maimon's friends—was far superior to that of the vast majority of the men who called themselves healers. And he also had to be aware of the high fees paid to doctors by members of the court and rich merchants, resulting sometimes in the accumulation of vast wealth not infrequently amounting in twenty-first-century terms to tens of millions of dollars. Already well known to both the Jewish and Muslim communities of Egypt, he had accepted the position of *rosh ab bet-din*, the presiding judge of the country's rabbinical court, which added to his prominence. He now had to be very practical—with his undoubted skill, his great reputation as a scholar, and the connections he had made with prominent Muslim colleagues, there was a good chance that he might become physician to high-ranking members of the caliph's retinue, with all the financial compensation that came with such appointments.

The previous several centuries had witnessed the ascendancy of Arab and Persian culture. In every sphere, Islamic thinkers and doers had made themselves heir to the accomplishments of the Greeks, brought them forward into the contemporary setting, and enlarged on them. They assimilated everything accessible that came before, whether Egyptian, Jewish, Greek, or Indian. In literature, in philosophy, and in mathematics, great contributions were being made by brilliant men, often with the patronage of the court and others of great wealth. Libraries, schools, observatories, and hospitals were built as an outgrowth of the intellectual ferment that characterized that long period of prosperity that followed the Arab conquests.

But in no area was the excitement as great as it was in science. The Muslim ruling class took great interest in the attempt to advance knowledge in such areas as astronomy and physics. This interest extended itself to medicine, so that major recognition was accorded to the leaders of the profession. Interestingly, real progress in medicine was rare during the Islamic period, the eagerness for learning manifesting itself more as a thirst for knowledge of physiology and the healing methods described by the Greeks. The Islamic medical writings were for the most part variations, interpretations, and modest expansions of the classical period, but this in itself was of major importance because Arabic texts became the repository for Greek medicine and science, which would otherwise likely have been lost. Thanks to Muslim culture, their value continued to be recognized during the long centuries that have become known as the Dark Ages for non-Arabic Europe.

And so, when Maimonides turned his thoughts to the practice of medicine in 1175, he was entering a field held in high regard, at a time when Arabic healing was at the height of its influence. He was bringing to it the advantages of his long years of study; his virtually photographic memory; his wide knowledge of philosophy and science and the rational approach to evidence they had taught him; and the wisdom and compassion for God's creatures that were so much a part of his Jewish heritage and his personal faith. But he could not have known that his years of being a healer and an author of medical treatises would elevate him to a level of such professional prominence that his name in future generations would be linked with those of Avicenna, Rhazes, and Averroës.

# The *Mishneh Torah*

Maimonides began his medical practice at a time of great change in Egypt. Having abolished the Fatimid caliphate in 1171 and declared the dominance of Sunnism, Saladin was the undisputed ruler of the country, taking on the title of sultan, although he would nominally be a subject of Nureddin until the latter's death in 1174.

No matter its political implications, Saladin's restoration of Sunni dominance arose out of a religious commitment that underlay many of the decisions he would make during the two decades when he was the most powerful leader in the Arab world. Raised in a prominent Kurdish family that had emigrated to Syria near the time of his birth in 1137—making him almost an exact contemporary of Maimonides—Saladin's interests as a young man had been more in the study of Islam than in the affairs of state. Even after joining his uncle's staff, he continued to be guided by his conviction of the importance of promoting the spread of the faith and the growth of its institutions, such as mosques and theological academies. Even when he began to expand the regions of his power, it was always with the underlying motive of fostering a religious renewal that would cleanse his people and enable them to regain the burgeoning vitality that had characterized their first centuries of rapid attainment.

To accomplish the goals he had set for himself, Saladin embraced the Islamic precept of jihad. Jihad is a campaign to advance the principles and hegemony of Islam, whether within one's own heart, by a relentless effort to convince others, or by doing battle with perceived enemies of the faith. Although in practice the duty of jihad has been invoked in every century to justify wars and terrorism whose basis is really political, the interweaving of religious doctrine, even if secondarily, is always meant to be a factor.

To Saladin, jihad meant propagation of the faith through any and all means necessary, whether it be by personal spiritual purification, the encouragement of scholarship, the building of institutions, or the waging of holy war. When conducting a military campaign, he attempted, insofar as possible, to follow principles articulated but rarely implemented by all three of the major faiths of the time: the avoidance of unnecessary violence on noncombatants and a minimization of the inevitable havoc that victorious armies so often wreak on their defeated enemies. These were the principles for which he would be remembered by history, and honored even by those whom he had conquered.

In practice, subjugated unbelievers who refused to accept

the true religion might be treated in a variety of ways, determined by the Muslim authority ruling the area where they lived. Though Christians and Jews were accorded special treatment because of the beliefs they shared with Islam, they nevertheless were considered infidels, and attempts were made to have them embrace the newer religion. Depending on the ruler—with the Almohads and Saladin personifying the two extremes—those who refused might be slaughtered or merely made to accept Islamic suzerainty and pay a special tax.

No sooner had Saladin taken over the government of Egypt than he began to plan ways to separate his kingdom from Syria. He saw his chance when Nureddin died in 1174, leaving his eleven-year-old son, Salih Ismail, as sultan, with a weak regent to govern in his name. In the confusion and virtual anarchy that followed, several of the Syrian states declared their independence, and the emir of Aleppo kidnapped the boy. To the Frankish king Amalric, this seemed the ideal opportunity to invade Syria and then Egypt. But in the final episode of the series of similar events that benefited Saladin, Amalric unexpectedly died, leaving a leprous thirteen-year-old son and a regent to govern.

Both Syria and the Kingdom of Jerusalem were thus in the hands of regents, but the Frankish regent, Baldwin, remained intent on conquering Syria, as did the emir of Aleppo. When he received a message from Damascus appealing for help, Saladin was only too pleased to cooperate. Moving as quickly as possible, he led a small army of only seven hundred horsemen across the desert and entered the city to the cheers of its thronging populace. Proceeding to take over the areas that had declared their independence, he quickly became the de facto ruler of all Egypt and now most of Syria as well. But Aleppo and Mosur remained a threat, and they allied themselves against him. Although he defeated their combined forces in April 1175, he allowed them to remain outside of the kingdom that he then declared. Twelve years later, he would defeat the Christian forces of the Kingdom of Jerusalem in a great battle and would overrun almost all of Palestine. Unlike the cataclysm of slaughter and rape let loose on both Muslims and Jews when the Christians conquered Jerusalem almost ninety years earlier, the entry of Saladin's army into the city was marked by the restraint and mercy that characterized his entire military career.

Saladin's decision to transfer his kingdom's capital from Damascus to Cairo in 1176 had salutory and perhaps life-saving consequences for Maimonides. The position of *nagid* had been usurped by an unscrupulous man named Zuta, who used his position to demand bribes and acquire considerable wealth. At great personal risk, Maimonides had become one of the leaders of the opposition to Zuta, resulting in his denunciation by the *nagid* and danger to his life. Some accounts tell of his having to flee the city for a while and seek refuge in a cave. But matters changed when he and his fellow protesters were able to utilize Saladin's return to Cairo as an opportunity to convince the ruler to depose the *nagid*, abolish the office, and move the exilarch from Damascus to his new capital.

*Exilarch* (in Hebrew, *resh galuta*, meaning "head of the Diaspora") was a title given to the political and judicial leader of the Jewish community outside of Jerusalem, dating back to the second century C.E. Claiming direct descent from King David, as had his forebears, the present exilarch, Judah ben Josiah, was a wise and judicious man who was well aware that Maimonides had by this time established himself as the leading Jewish scholar in Egypt and had become very highly regarded because of his letter to the Yemenites and his *Commentary on the Mishnah*. He may also have been aware that Moses had for some six years been at work on another great treatise, to be called the *Mishneh Torah*. One of Judah's first official acts was to declare that all of Moses's decrees in religious matters were to be considered final, going so far as to countersign them himself. This meant that Maimonides was now the spiritual leader of all Jews in Saladin's kingdom.

Maimonides wasted no time in resuming his campaign against the heresy of the Karaites. Joined by nine other scholars, he issued an edict declaring that married women who used the Karaite rite to purify themselves after menstruation—and this seems to have been true of many who otherwise adhered to traditional Judaism—were disobeying the rules set down by the sages of the Talmud, and should therefore be divorced and lose the dowry they had brought to the marriage. This caused major practical difficulties for such women and brought a large number back into the fold. Over the succeeding decades, this deliberately harsh regulation contributed to the disappearance of the Karaites from the Arab lands, though conversion to Islam was probably even more of a factor.

It was also in this period that Maimonides undertook to fulfill a halakhic obligation from which he would not consider exempting himself, that every Jew make a copy of the Torah. He worked from a highly regarded Masoretic text that had been brought to Egypt for safekeeping when the Crusaders were murdering the Jews of Jerusalem and destroying their homes and synagogues. Although the Maimonidean scroll has long been lost, the most remarkable thing about it was not any stylistic or graphologic characteristic but the mere fact that a man whose medical practice was beginning to grow; who was receiving increasing numbers of inquiries from afar that needed responsa; who was constantly being consulted on matters of Law and life by members of his own community; who pored over scripture and commentary at every available moment; who was supplementing his income by lecturing on philosophy and science; who treated every obligation as though it was the only one he had—that such a man somehow found time to copy the Torah, a project that must be carried out with scrupulous attention to detail lest the most minute error render it impure and therefore useless.

And during all of this, Moses was applying himself to the second of the three great works of his life, the *Mishneh Torah*, a huge project he would not complete until 1180, ten years after its inception.

The title of the treatise *Mishneh Torah* means "second Torah" (alternatively, "repetition of the Torah"), and its fourteen volumes, consisting of eighty-six monographs divided into one thousand chapters, were conceived with the purpose of allowing readers to go directly to any aspect of the Oral Law without having to deal with the abstruse, tortuous, unorganized, disputatious, and sometimes internally contradictory Talmud and later responsa and commentaries added by the *geonim* (plural of *gaon*, meaning renowned rabbinic leader) between the sixth and eleventh centuries, to which there was no order or system. As he would later explain in a letter to his most esteemed pupil, Joseph ibn Aknin, in 1190, Moses originally embarked on the project as a sort of digest for his own use, "that I should not be compelled to search all of Talmudic literature for particular material." As the writing proceeded, he came to realize that such a work might serve all Jews, because there existed no code of law "presenting the decisions without controversy and errors." What was needed was a single, well-organized, systematic source—omitting the circuitous discussions, obscure references, and tangential asides—a book to which anyone could turn for rapid resolution of points of law.

In our days when scholars are few and scholarship rare, I, Moses, the son of Maimon the Spaniard, am compiling a book on the entire Jewish Law without discussions or debates, wherein all the laws are clearly explained.

It was the author's intent that henceforth it would not be necessary to consult any other source than the Torah and his own *Mishneh Torah*. Maimonides was writing what many have called a constitution for the Jewish state that he envisioned as being on the horizon. The treatise was to be accessible, fluent, and as concise as was consistent with completeness. Everything would be there, without a single unnecessary word, reference, or adornment—and all available to a reader in the flip of a few pages.

But before embarking on this massive undertaking, Maimonides set about writing a preliminary work in Arabic, called *Sefer ha-Mitzvot*, or Book of Commandments. The Talmud refers to a total of 613 commandments decreed by God in the Pentateuch, to be followed by all Jews every day of their lives. But the list had become far longer than that over the years, with considerable confusion existing over which commandments were the correct ones. Maimonides now reviewed them all and specified those 613 that were to be considered valid. It was only after completing this project that he felt prepared to go on to his codification of all the Law, considering *Sefer ha-Mitzvot* to be an introductory volume to the larger work.

That Maimonides believed the arrival of the Messiah to be near is obvious from others of his writings. It will be recalled that his *Letter to Yemen* gave an actual date of 4976, or 1216 C.E., for the return of prophecy that would precede the great coming. Although he claimed to have derived this from an old family tradition, conditions in the late twelfth century seemed consistent with the dire situation in which the Jews were predicted to be in the years before being saved. The persecutions in France, Germany, and most of the Muslim world; the rising power of Christianity and Islam; and the clash of the two major religions—all of these fit into the foretold patterns. No wonder that a false herald had appeared in Yemen, among other places; it was a messianic age, and Maimonides' conviction of immanence was widely shared.

This meant that the Jews were destined soon to return to Palestine under the leadership of a human descendant of the House of David—as Maimonides himself was thought to be—who would be the wisest man to appear on earth since the great prophet Moses the Lawgiver. The Jewish nation would therefore need a set of precepts equivalent to a constitution, and it should be based on the Torah. Such a constitution would declare the principles of Judaism, classifying and codifying its laws without the necessity of reiterating how they came to be. The *Mishneh Torah* was meant to be that constitution.

And it was also meant to respond to a problem, stated clearly by Maimonides, that had long cried out for a solution. Knowledge of the wisdom of the sages was fading from the minds of far too many members of the Jewish community, not only in the Arabic-speaking lands but in Europe as well.

> In our days, severe vicissitudes prevail, and all feel the pressure of hard times. The wisdom of our wise men has disappeared; the understanding of our prudent men is hidden. Hence the commentaries of the Geonim and their compilation of laws and responses, which they took care to make clear, have in our times become hard to understand, so that only a few individuals properly comprehend them. . . . On these grounds, I Moses the son of Maimon the Spaniard, bestirred myself . . . [to compose a work from which] the entire Oral Law might become systematically known to all.

Moreover, contemporary study of Jewish knowledge and Law was fragmented by rivalries and uncertainty about the relative importance of differing and sometimes competing customs.

Not only the depleted state of scholarship demanded addressing. The very conditions under which the harassed Jews of the period were forced to live presented another factor. "We have come upon hard and evil days," Maimonides had written in the *Letter to Yemen*, "and have not abided in tranquility; we are weary and given no rest. How then shall halakha become clear to one who wanders from city to city and kingdom to kingdom?"

The twelfth century was a time not unlike the era when

Judah ha-Nasi undertook to write down the Mishnah, stated Maimonides in the introduction to his *Mishneh Torah*, a time when "the disciples were becoming fewer and new troubles were coming upon them, and the Roman Empire was expanding and growing stronger, and Jews were wandering away to the ends of the earth." His was an enterprise, he was certain, that had to be undertaken.

The *Mishneh Torah* has been called *Yad ha-Hazakah* (The Strong Hand), from the final verse of the Torah, "By the strong hand and awesome power that Moses performed before all Israel" (Deuteronomy 34:12). The term may also allude secondarily to the formula that Jews customarily proclaim in the synagogue when the reading of the last words of a book of the Pentateuch are completed, "*Hazak! Hazak! V'nit'hazeik!* (Be strong! Be strong! And may we be strengthened!). Hebrew letters may also be used as numbers, and the word *Yad* is equivalent to fourteen, the number of books into which Maimonides (who was born on the fourteenth of the Hebrew month of Nisan) divided his great work, sometimes uncomfortably cramming topics together in order to accomplish his aim.

Unlike the *Commentary*, which was written in Judeo-Arabic, the *Mishneh Torah* was written entirely in a form of Hebrew similar to that of the Mishnah. It would thus be directly available without need for translation to Jews everywhere, and not only to those living in Islamic lands. The decision to write for all Jews revealed Maimonides' awareness of his growing reputation, and no doubt his determination to make his influence spread even wider. Within a few decades, the *Mishneh Torah* would enhance and universalize his image, bringing him recognition as the leading religious authority of the worldwide Jewish community. Its style is conversational and pleasing, and yet characterized by a terseness and precision consistent with Maimonides' statement, "If I had been able to put all of the Oral Law into one chapter, I would not have used two."

> All our works are carefully sifted and cleansed. It is never our intention to swell the volume of our writings. . . . When we have to explain a topic, we only explain that which is absolutely in need of explanation. . . . Outside of this, we usually confine ourselves in our writings to a brief exposition of the subject.

As might be imagined, it proved impossible for a scholar with Maimonides' breadth of learning and interests to adhere strictly to his aim of brevity, a fact that actually benefited the literary quality of the work. But he did as well as he could, going directly—without any superfluous comment—to the legal decisions he deemed most appropriate for each circumstance. These legal decisions sometimes differed from those of his rabbinic predecessors. He did not see fit to clutter his text by naming sources or describing the controversies or reasoning that had gone into the Talmudic precepts on which he commented or rendered judgment. The judgments, in fact, were his own, and they were based not only on the Oral Law but sometimes on his knowledge of philosophy, science, commerce, and the societal needs of the times. He did not hesitate to incorporate his wide understanding of non-Jewish sources, such as geometry and other mathematics, astronomy, medical literature, and the writings of classical philosophers, most particularly Aristotle. For him to do this was only natural, considering his conviction that faith and reason not only can exist in harmony but should be brought together in order to find universal truth. In fact, when certain of the Talmudic precepts that he considered questionable were contrary to his certainty in the understanding of science and of reason, he omitted them unless they concerned crucial and well-accepted concepts.

Although a highly personal testament, the *Mishneh Torah* was also a universal and authoritative statement of how a Jew should live his life and worship his God. Written in the clear and elegant Hebrew that made it a literary triumph as well as a theologic and legalistic one, the work did a great deal to encourage stylistic improvements in the language. But most important, the fourteen books were destined to exert a profound influence on rabbinic thought and Jewish life for centuries. In terms of Talmudic studies, it became— after the Talmud itself—the most important and influential work yet written after the destruction of the Second Temple, and it has remained so until the present day, although its strictly codifying aspects have been displaced by the digested halakhic text called the Shulhan Arukh (Prepared Table), written by the compiler Joseph Caro in the sixteenth century, itself much influenced by its Maimonidean predecessor.

The *Mishneh Torah* accomplished two ends. It compiled and codified all the halakha while making the Law not only clear but comprehensible as a reasonable approach to living and to the understanding of God. Moreover, it addressed contemporary concerns while it provided a guide to Jewish living for all future years. In this, it had about it the aura of timelessness. Maimonides did all of this within an entirely new system of categorization, so unique to his own intellect that the authors of later canonical codes—Jacob ben Asher, Joseph Caro, and Moses Isserles—did not use it.

To a modern reader, certain passages of the *Mishneh Torah* have an uncommonly relevant tone, resonating as they do with social, economic, and theological issues that still concern us today. Beyond strictly ritualistic matters, it is a treatise on ethics, as conceived by a mind steeped in religious law, classical philosophy, medical healing of body and mind, and a commitment to personal morality. It is a work of compassion redolent of the ancient Jewish commandment of *tzedakah*, charity in the broadest sense of beneficence to others.

And those others are not only Jews but all people. Maimonides makes it clear that the indigent of every belief, including heathens, must be cared for, be comforted in their times of mourning and affliction, and have their dead buried. Asked for his general feelings about gentiles and their eligibility for an afterlife, Maimonides would later express his opinion in one of his responsa, consistent with the tenor of the *Mishneh Torah:* "Know that the Lord desires the heart, and that the intention of the heart is the measure of all things. That is why the Sages say, 'The pious among the Gentiles have a share in *Olam ha-Ba*, the World-to-Come.' "

The honor and dignity of individuals are sacred, declared Maimonides in the *Mishneh Torah*, and must not be violated under any circumstances, whether those individuals be free men or slaves. The reputation of others is to be protected, whether from outright slander or from damaging insinuation. Maimonides considered violation of this precept sufficient reason for a man to be denied his share of *Olam ha-Ba*.

Maimonides insists that *tzedakah* must be a motivating force in the life of every Jew, not only in the form of monetary charity, but as social justice, benevolent deeds, and ordinary kindness. And the *tzedakah* is to be dispensed in such a way that the beneficiary is not degraded by accepting it, that is, it must be given with an open heart and an open hand. "Whoever gives alms to the poor with bad grace and a downcast look," wrote Maimonides, "loses all the merit of his action though he bestow a thousand gold pieces."

But his emphasis on the dignity of the individual does not lessen the importance of community that Maimonides taught as not only a precept but a bounden duty. Each of us has obligations to our fellow human beings that cannot be fulfilled without active participation in the society of which we are part, he wrote. Isolation from others is indifference to their needs and to the needs of the entire congregation of Israel and the people in it. Separation from the larger group is such a serious misdeed, Maimonides taught, that it is punishable by losing one's portion in *Olam ha-Ba*.

Even self-chosen isolation for the purpose of study and holiness is viewed with disfavor. One should live in the real world as did the rabbinic sages of Israel in the past, for the real world is not unholy. Only by participating in it can one attend to the needs of others and the greater society. Among the needs of others is that one should not be a burden on them by becoming a public charge; it is incumbent on each Jew to earn a living. And the needs of others also include not taking advantage of them by profiting excessively from business or engaging in practices that restrain anyone's freedom to earn. Maimonides had particularly harsh words for fraudulent practices, such as inaccurate scales: "The punishment for incorrect measures is more severe than the punishment for immorality, for the latter is a sin against God only, the former against one's fellow man."

Jacob Minkin, a twentieth-century author, has written a single paragraph that well describes the contents of the *Mishneh Torah*. The following is from his *World of Moses Maimonides, with Selections from His Writings*, published in 1987. Like virtually all authors, Minkin refers to the work as the Code:

> Maimonides' Code is an encyclopedia of Jewish philosophy, theology, ethics, and ritual. It is also a treatise

on commerce, industry, finance, property, inheritance, taxation, legal procedure, and penal law. It is a law book whose domain extends over almost every form of human activity. It legislates for the scholar, it provides for the trader, and prescribes for the shopkeeper. It seeks to guide and curb, to promote justice and restrain violence. It regards the simplest human activity and enterprise from the moral and ethical point of view. Its categorical imperative may be summed up in the words: "Act so as to find grace and favor in the eyes of God and man." Maimonides' Code secures the rights and privileges of the individual but holds the interests and welfare of society to be paramount in all things. Man may not be guided by his own likes and dislikes; he may not live, act, and behave as he will without squaring his conduct with the society and community in which he lives.

In much of this, Minkin might just as well have been describing the Talmud. But that was precisely the point. In ten years of work, Maimonides had accomplished the monumental task of presenting Talmudic teachings—brought up to contemporary time and adorned with the fruits of his unique intellect and broad knowledge of religious, philosophical, medical, and humanistic matters—in a concise, organized way that could be used with great efficiency and precision by any speaker of Hebrew seeking enlightenment in the Law of Judaism. Unlike the Talmud, the Code of Maimonides was a highly structured gem of summation. And it was a literary masterpiece. Its author had achieved his goal:

> To smooth the path, interpret, and, as we thought necessary, help those who could not understand the words of the Torah scholars, of blessed memory, who preceded us, to understand them. It seems to us that we brought closer and simplified abstruse and profound subjects; we collected and compiled subjects which were scattered and dispersed; and we knew, at any rate, that we were achieving something valuable. For if the case was as we thought it to be, then by simplifying, facilitating, and compiling, in a manner that none of our predecessors had ever done, we have already achieved something by benefitting people and have earned divine recompense.

As with the *Commentary on the Mishnah*, Moses hardly expected that his *Mishneh Torah* would meet with universal approval, and he was, of course, correct. The criticisms came from a variety of sources, ranging from those with legitimate disagreements over certain of its premises and presumptions to those whose attacks were of a more personal nature, and sometimes even vituperative. With the publication of this work, Moses had become the most eminent Jewish scholar in the world. Even those who had not previously acknowledged him now had to accept his intellectual and spiritual leadership. To the great majority of Jews who were familiar with his teachings, the treatise only reinforced what they already knew of him. But to those resentful of his religious authority, the *Mishneh Torah* provided an opportunity for attack.

The most serious of the criticisms did have some validity. This was the perception on the part of some scholars that Maimonides intended his work to displace the Talmud. He had, in fact, left himself open to such a charge in the closing words of his introduction: "I called the name of this work *Mishneh Torah*, for all that a man has to do is to read first the Written Law [Torah] and follow it up by this work, and he will know the entire Oral Law without the need of reading any other work between them."

To this accusation, Maimonides replied that his intention had been quite the opposite. By spreading knowledge of the Talmud, he said, the *Mishneh Torah* would lead readers to undertake in-depth study of its complexities. Whatever else the Code was, it was meant as a guide through the thickets of Oral Law, one that might stimulate those who sought greater detail to turn to the earlier work for more complete enlightenment. Nowhere, he pointed out, does he assert that the Talmud should be abandoned.

Other criticisms were equally understandable. Some were theological, but others fall into the category of an author not having written the book that certain readers wanted. There were strenuous objections to the absence of references; to certain philosophical or scientific speculations that were the inimitable mark of his wide-ranging intellect but seen by some as secular contamination; to his occasional contradictions of the decisions made centuries earlier by the Talmudic sages; to his insistence, despite widespread belief to the contrary, on the incorporeality of God (he went so far as to use the word *heretic* to describe Jews who believed otherwise); to his attacks on witchcraft and superstitious practices; to his assertion that the rewards of *Olam ha-Ba* are to be spiritual rather than physical; and, finally, to a certain note of rationalism throughout the text, denoting his commitment to explain events in terms of observable phenomena rather than by miraculous intercession.

To a modern reader, there is one criticism of the *Mishneh Torah* that must stand out as does no other, for time has shown it to be a matter of great concern: The apprehension was expressed by some scholars of the time that codifying Jewish law in such a highly structured manner would stifle the innovation that had until then characterized Judaism. The Oral Law itself had come into existence through constant reinterpretations of Torah and early commentary, serving to mold a flexible faith responsive to the needs of its era. The Talmud, in fact, by emphasizing discussion and debate, showed how it was possible to view matters of ritual and personal conduct from various perspectives. Ironically, one of the merits of the *Mishneh Torah* was that it stood as a document of the twelfth century, bringing decisions forward to be appropriate for that era. And yet, by its very existence—and by its being the result of the uncontested judgments of a single man, no matter his wisdom—it risked ossifying the law into a changeless pattern that allowed no innovation. The fear was that Judaism would be frozen in time. Maimonides had written a constitution without mechanisms for amendments except those that he himself continued to write for the rest of his life, in the form of responsa and direct revisions, as he constantly reviewed and made small changes in his great work. But if he was writing a constitution that remained open-ended as long as he lived, there was no Supreme Court to adjudicate disputes that might arise concerning its interpretation.

It is impossible to believe that Moses did not think long and hard about this unintended consequence of his great treatise. Or was it, in fact, as unintended as might be thought? He was, after all, writing a constitution for a Jewish state that he believed to be imminent, a Jewish state ruled by an all-knowing and long-lived Messiah whose successors would be Davidic descendants as close to the will of God as he. In such a paradisiacal place, there would be no change, for all was and would be, by definition, perfect. If Maimonides is to be believed—if his sincerity is to be accepted—in predicting the imminent coming of the Messiah, he was writing for a changeless eternity.

The criticisms of the Code, while usually couched in the measured language of scholars, did sometimes reach a level of ad hominem harshness that betrayed the resentment behind them. These came from men who thought of themselves as rivals to Maimonides, or even as his betters, attacking what they considered his presumptuousness in daring to create a definitive code of law. Not only that, but such an influential book having been written in Hebrew meant that its author achieved a universal fame and authority in all Jewish communities within a relatively short time of its availability. Even as important a work as the *Commentary on the Mishnah* had not had this effect because its Arabic language made it inaccessible to the Jews living in Christian lands.

Some were threatened by the Code in other ways. It was reported that certain judges were displeased with its wide availability because halakhic matters would now become easy for ordinary citizens to check. In that era of few highly qualified experts in the Law, such men must have feared second-guessing or perhaps the possibility of being exposed as less skilled than had been thought.

Chief among those whose resentments boiled up after the appearance of the *Mishneh Torah* was the *gaon* of Baghdad, Samuel ibn Ali, a man whose approach to leadership of the Jewish community differed radically from that of Maimonides. Ibn Ali's rancorous dispute with the man who would later be named *nagid* of Egypt would go on for years and become a source of considerable anguish for Maimonides, try as he might to treat the contentiousness of his antagonist with restraint and even respect.

"*Nagid*" was one of several titles designating the head of the Jewish community in the countries of what is now called the Middle East, where they had a significant degree of self-rule. Palestine and Persia were governed by a *nasi* (prince) and a *resh galuta* (exilarch) respectively (see p. 103). Syria and Mesopotamia were also governed by an exilarch, a term dating back to the Babylonian captivity but having essentially the same meaning as the later *nagid*, a title thought to have been introduced in tenth-century Egypt (see p. 55). Baghdad, in addition to its exilarch, had also the religious leader called the *gaon*. Although Samuel ibn Ali was the *gaon*, he was far from being a spiritual man. Living in a luxurious palace and served by sixty slaves, he had taken over all power when the exilarch died in 1175. Despite great learning, he rejected the modesty expected of a religious leader, being at most times not only attended by several of the slaves but often trailed by a retinue of subordinate judges. Legend has it that from a golden throne he lectured to large groups of students who came to him from all parts of the Jewish world.

Determined to assert hegemony over all the world's Jews, ibn Ali considered Maimonides a dangerous rival, doing what he could to find causes for conflict with him. Although this might be in the form of disagreeing with his judgments in disputes of the Law, the publication of the *Mishneh Torah* provided the ideal opportunity to mount a strong campaign whose intent was to diminish Maimonides in the eyes of his followers. Because others also disagreed with various aspects of the Code, and some of them resented Maimonides as much as did Samuel, the *gaon* had some vociferous allies.

The most serious charge made by ibn Ali and others against Maimonides was an unrestrained attack on his doctrine concerning resurrection. In reply, Maimonides outlined his statements once more and perhaps relented just a bit in certain respects lest anyone continue to construe that he did not believe in the concept, a position that would seem to violate essential Talmudic teachings. In his usual temperate way, Maimonides tried to stay aloof from the vituperation that was being flung at him, going so far as to gently rebuke several of his disciples who had responded harshly to ibn Ali's charges. But the maliciousness of ibn Ali and his allies nevertheless took a toll. It is in this period, when Moses was just past the age of fifty, that one first begins to read of a recurrence of the otherwise unspecified "heart trouble" that had first appeared during his depression and would intermittently plague him for the rest of his life, eventually claiming him.

The conflict with ibn Ali would go on for years before it finally ended in Maimonides' favor. His reputation throughout the Jewish world was by that time so assured that even a figure as powerful as the Baghdad *gaon* could not sully it. Not only had Maimonides been vindicated by the arguments and support of so many scholars, but the status of the *Mishneh Torah* had soon become unquestioned as the ultimate source of authority on Jewish law, after the Talmud itself. But the clashes with ibn Ali caused the Rambam so much vexation that he is said to have succumbed to a period of major illness after one of the particularly contentious episodes of dispute, and to have remained sick for many months afterward.

Soon after its completion, the *Mishneh Torah* became widely available. The criticisms notwithstanding, acceptance of the book as the ultimate authoritative source was rapid and widespread. Hundreds of copyists soon were occupied in supplying the demand for it, and the name of Maimonides penetrated far and wide into every corner of the Jewish world. Before long, few matters of Jewish law were discussed without turning to the pages of the *Mishneh Torah* to seek guidance from the master. Even today, when disagreements arise among the learned, it is not uncommon to see one or another of the scholarly disputants pull down from the shelf a volume of his own well-worn copy of the great Code, with the comment, "Let's see what the Rambam has to say."

# The Guide for the Perplexed

It was probably in 1175, when he was thirty-eight years old, that Maimonides married for what may have been the second time. Some authorities believe that he had been wed while quite young but that his wife died shortly afterward, during the family's wanderings. There is, in fact, no basis for such a belief and certainly not a shred of real evidence that justifies it. It may simply be that those who subscribe to the story prefer to believe that such a great sage of Judaism would not wait until so late to give up his bachelor existence. Hebraic scholars have traditionally married young, with leadership in the community being barred to those still without a wife, except under unusual circumstances. For some students of the Rambam's life, it may be unpalatable to think of him as unmarried until his thirty-ninth year.

The woman Moses now chose (whose name is lost to history) was the daughter of a rabbi, Mishael Halevi, and the sister of Abu'l Maa'ali (whose Hebrew name was Uziel), one of the royal scribes who would later become the husband of the older of Moses's sisters. As far as can be told, this was

Maimonides' first connection to the court, and it was a good one, because the person for whom the scribe worked was one of Saladin's wives and is thought to have been the mother of the successor to his throne, al Afdal. It is uncertain whether this relationship helped Maimonides in his struggles with Zuta, but it was certainly influential in his later securing a post as physician to the court.

Because a marriage criterion for men of his scholarly attainment would certainly have been the wife's ability to bear children, we can assume that Maimonides' bride must have been in her early twenties at most, and very likely her late teens. Still, several years seem to have passed before the couple had a little girl. She died early, as so many infants did until little more than a century ago, and it was not until 1186 that a son, Abraham, was born. From his birth, the forty-eight-year-old father lavished on this boy all the loving attention that he had once devoted to his adored brother, David. As Maimon had been to Moses, he became Abraham's primary source of learning; he would see to it that the boy became acquainted not only with the literature and customs of Judaism, but also that he obtained the training in science and philosophy that had been so vital a part of his own education.

By now it has become apparent to any but the most hasty reader of these pages that very little information is provided here about the women in the life of Maimonides. Although his books, essays, and letters are written in a highly personal style and sometimes reveal a great deal about the conditions in which he lived, Moses wrote virtually nothing about any female influence or person. It is known that one of his sisters was named Miriam, but the names of his mother, his other sister, and his wife do not appear in any communication written by himself or by others, and scant biographic detail about them has ever been found. The reason for these omissions will come as no surprise to those familiar with the period and with the role assigned to women in the contemporary Jewish family.

Neither prayer nor scholarship was asked of women of the time beyond what was needed to perform or oversee household rituals, and perhaps keep up with the synagogue service in which they might participate from a balcony or from behind a thick curtain. No scholarly tractate, letter, or communication of any kind would be likely to mention them except in obliquities. Although women were honored as the foundation of the family, they trod lightly so as not to disturb the meditations of the men to whom their lives were dedicated.

In a role that was both peripheral to the world of men and central to its continuity, wives were spoken of as though in the abstract. In letters, for example, it was not customary to ask after their welfare, for that might imply a prurient interest. In the Book of Holiness of the *Mishneh Torah*, Maimonides wrote, "A man may not inquire after the well-being of a woman at all, not even through a messenger." Instead, a correspondent would write something like "I hope the health of your house has been good," where "house" was understood to mean wife. It is a very telling choice of words, and the reason is simply that anything to do with the house is hers to supervise. His wife was indeed a man's house. Without her, his scholarly needs would have no roof or walls to protect them, and his mind would not be free to roam far in the precincts of holiness and the Law.

We know about such letters in the same way that we know so much of the narrative of the Rambam's life. Over the centuries, particularly in the past 150 years, it has been possible to piece together the general outline of his biography—and some of the specifics—by study of original or more often copied manuscripts that have turned up in such sources as royal or private collections that through the years became part of the great libraries of Judaica in the United States, Russia, and other continental European countries, Britain, Palestine, and then Israel. In certain of the libraries translations have been found from Maimonides' original Judaeo-Arabic into Hebrew of letters and other manuscripts that scholars can with a high degree of confidence attribute to him. Similar articles have been found in the Rambam's own hand or written by his scribes and signed by him. Another source of his letters and short treatises are books written by slightly later authors, into which his words have been copied; in these cases, the material has been reliably identified by such an author as having been of Maimonidean composition. Most or all of the lengthy letters and treatises were preserved in these ways, but fragments of the originals as well as some short letters written in Maimonides' own hand have also turned up in the Cairo *Genizah*. Some of these fragments are biographical, and some are bits of treatises that were more fully preserved in other manuscripts. Further, unverified letters have been discovered both in and out of the *Genizah*, as to whose authenticity scholars disagree. Using criteria of style and (for the handwritten ones) criteria of form, pieces from the various sources that are attributed to him are virtually certain to be authentic, by scholarly agreement. In addition to these direct sources, knowledge of the events and of the Rambam's role in them comes in much smaller part from certain letters written by Arab authors of the time or slightly thereafter.

Mention has just been made of the *Genizah*, which is a story in itself. The word means "depository," but it is a depository of a special sort, one in which is stored materials that are inscribed with any reference to God. Because Jewish law prohibits the discarding of such artifacts, it was the custom for centuries to bury them or stow them away in the structure or attics of synagogues. Returning from one of several journeys to the Middle East in 1896, two widowed sisters, Mrs. Lewis and Mrs. Gibson, familiar with classical languages—Hebrew, Arabic, and Aramaic—brought back to England a fragment of manuscript they had obtained in Cairo. The origin was the *Genizah*, a room in the women's gallery of the Ben Ezra Synagogue in Fustat, built in 882.

They showed it to their friend Dr. Solomon Schechter, Reader in Rabbinics at Cambridge University, who identified it as a tenth-century copy of the original Hebrew manuscript of the book of the Apocrypha called Ecclesiasticus. Schechter traveled to Cairo, consulted with its Jewish community, and obtained their permission to bring almost all of the *Genizah*'s contents, more than 100,000 manuscript fragments of paper, cloth, vellum, and papyrus, back to Cambridge as a gift from them. Other bits made their way to libraries in various parts of the world. The pieces proved to include not only sacred writings from the tenth to the fifteenth centuries but also secular materials—some in Arabic—that had been indiscriminately deposited there from the libraries and collections of Jewish Cairenes. The *Genizah* fragments have been an invaluable source of information about Jewish and Arab life during the five-hundred-year period from which they originate. Though the specifically Maimonidean materials are relatively few, they have added to the knowledge of the Rambam's life. The *Genizah* materials, most of which are written in Judeao-Arabic, have also proven to be a rich source for elucidating the Arab and Jewish medicine of the period. Indirectly, they have shed light on the ways in which the work of Maimonides related to the medical profession of his time.

Like everything else he did, this unique doctor was meticulous in his studies of the human body and of the therapies that might heal when it became disordered. One can tell from reading his medical treatises that his knowledge of medicine was wide and his sagacity in dealing with individual patients remarkable. His frankness and honesty stood out in a time when so little of any therapeutic usefulness was known that charlatans abounded and glibness was often the most important ingredient in professional success.

Maimonides succeeded for other reasons. Once he had actually begun to practice medicine, he integrated the personal experience of sickness into the erudition that his wide reading of Arabic predecessors had given him. The result, after some years, was a mastery of medicine based on the two factors that have always been the ultimate basis for the most skillful medical care: the knowledge made available by a critical reading of the authoritative sources, and the bedside experience of a meticulous observer. Just as these would become the hallmarks of the medical writings he later undertook, they were—from the first—the key to his success as a practicing doctor.

That success came relatively soon after his practice began. Because he was already held in high regard by the Jews of Fustat, it was quite natural for people to come to Maimonides once he made it known that he was available for medical care. It was common, as noted earlier, for rabbis and scholars to be physicians during the medieval period, and more than a few of the Jewish doctors who attended Muslim or Christian rulers were also leaders in their own religious communities. When, in 1187, Saladin's vizier, el Fadil, developed a sickness that did not respond to the ministrations of the court physicians, Abu'l Maa'ali did not hesitate to suggest, probably through the wife of Saladin who employed him, that his brother-in-law be consulted.

El Fadil was so pleased with the care he received at the hands of his new doctor (and certainly with his rapid recovery) that he appointed Maimonides to be one of the court physicians, several of whom were Jews. The small salary that came with the position was far less important than the subsequent public recognition of his relationship with the vizier, which led to a significant expansion of his practice and a great increase in the number of Muslim families who asked for his services. As Saladin was so frequently engaged in military campaigns elsewhere, el Fadil was the most powerful man in the Muslim world. We know from his new physician's later writings that he was a man whose great learning and literary ability were matched by a charitable sense of responsibility to the people of Egypt. He supported institutions for the poor, built academies of learning, and was known for his public and private kindnesses to his subjects. It is for good reason that he and Maimonides so soon came to admire each other.

Shortly before these events took place, Maimonides began a relationship with a young scholar and physician named Joseph ibn Aknin, which would brighten his life in later years and prove an inspiration in his studies. Joseph, who lived in the Moroccan port city of Ceuta, was, like Moses, educated not only in religious matters but in medicine, science, mathematics, and philosophy. Also like Moses, he had suffered mightily at the hands of the Almohads. But conditions had become even worse in recent years, with the ascendance to power in 1184 of a new ruler who persecuted not only the practicing Jews but those who had become Muslims as well. Just when Joseph, living as a pseudo-convert, came to realize that he could no longer stay in Morocco, a copy of the *Mishneh Torah* came into his hands.

Like more than a few of the young Jewish intellectuals of the time, Joseph had been struggling to reconcile the teachings of the Bible and Talmud with his wide knowledge of philosophy and science. As he studied the pages of the *Mishneh Torah*, he realized that he had at last found the master who might help him make his way through the thickets of uncertainty and confusion. He determined to travel to Fustat, not only to seek out the great scholar, but also to enjoy the freedom that was in such abundance there.

Arriving first in Alexandria and lacking what he considered the audacity to go directly to Fustat, Joseph wrote to Maimonides asking to study with him. He included with the letter some samples of his own Hebrew and Arabic poetry. Maimonides had little use for poetry, but he recognized in the verse's thought and in the letter itself the mark of a powerful intellect and strong education. These were rare commodities among the Jews of Egypt, and Moses did not hesitate to suggest that Joseph become his student.

Joseph came to Fustat in 1185, and for the next two years he lived in the home of Maimonides. The men became far more than mere master and pupil. It would not be over-statement to say that the childless Maimonides soon came to think of his disciple as a son. In fact, when Abraham was born in 1186, the joyful father told his young pupil just that: He thought of each of them as his son. The two men studied everything together, both religious and secular. For both, it was a period of unsurpassed intellectual excitement. Not only did Joseph learn from his mentor, but he was able to be of service to him, assisting him in the community and occasionally traveling on his behalf.

At the end of two years, Joseph left Fustat and moved first to Aleppo and soon afterward to Baghdad. The reason for his departure is uncertain, but it may have been economic. Some accounts have him going to Baghdad to confront the region's *gaon*, Samuel ibn Ali, who, it will be recalled, had been a severe critic of Maimonides to the point of vicious assaults on his scholarship and integrity. Whatever the reason, Joseph's departure from Egypt did not sever the relationship with his beloved teacher; in some ways the distance strengthened it. From then on, the two scholars corresponded frequently, and continued to discuss in epistolary form the many vexations of reconciling the teachings of philosophy with the beliefs of Judaism. It was in response to these ongoing discussions that Maimonides, soon after Joseph left, began work on the treatise destined to become the most famous of his writings, *The Guide for the Perplexed:* "When, by the will of God, we parted and you went your way, our discussions aroused in me a resolution which had long been dormant. Your absence has prompted me to compose this treatise for you and for those who are like you, however few they may be."

It is in the words "however few they may be" that a clue may be found to a theme that runs throughout the non-medical writings of Maimonides. Beginning with the *Commentary on the Mishnah*, reference is made again and again to the differences in meaning derived from study of the Law between those understood by ordinary people and those accessible only to men enlightened by vast scholarship and study: Biblical and Talmudic stories, statements, the entire history of the world and the Jewish people from Genesis to Exodus—all of them must be viewed with an eye to allegory and metaphor. Literal interpretation, Maimonides believed, is only an adornment to attract those who are incapable of comprehending the complex truths that lie beneath. "Employ your reason," the Rambam exhorted those capable of doing so, "and you will be able to discern what is said allegorically, figuratively, and hyperbolically, and what is meant literally." The incorporeality of God, for example, or the nonphysical nature of the rewards in the world to come, are not concepts easily grasped by ordinary minds, and they must therefore be leavened by images visible to the imagination, or by tales consistent with the experience of everyday life, if the people are to be drawn to faith. But spiritual riches await the few who are capable of grappling with far greater themes, and it is for them that such works as the *Guide* were written. It is for this reason that controversy greeted so much of Maimonides' ouevre, and not only the resentment of those who considered themselves his rivals.

> After all, I am a man who—if the subject urges him, if the road is too narrow for him, and if he knows no other way to teach a proven truth except by appealing to one chosen man, even if failing to appeal to ten thousand fools—prefers imparting the truth to this one man. I do not heed the complaints of the greater crowd, and I wish to wrest the one chosen man from his irresoluteness and show him the way out of his perplexity so that he may become perfect and sound.

The *Guide*'s introduction, from which this statement comes, is largely an explanation of intent and method, and one cannot help but wonder whether it is also a statement of the seemingly unresolvable conflict between faith and reason that Maimonides faced throughout his own life. Once a man has been exposed to the evidence of science and the methodology of logic, the Rambam wrote, he will remain restless even though—in the interest of maintaining his religious convictions—he rejects what he has learned from the philosophers and observers of nature; his unease will annoyingly persist until he can find some concordance that will ease the niggling residuum of doubt from which he cannot rid himself. That *The Guide for the Perplexed* is, despite its author's learning and brilliance, an imperfect solution to the dilemma may only mean that a perfect one will never be found, may only mean that these two ways of viewing the universe and humankind are best brought together by seeking those swaths of common ground along which both can progress, rather than by attempting to intertwine their respective footsteps on a single path to truth or by outrightly rejecting one for the other. This is precisely the goal that Maimonides pursued in writing the *Guide*—to demonstrate, to the relatively few who were qualified to understand it, that, far more often than might be imagined, faith and reason can be shown to share common ground and similar perspectives. While the uninitiated see vast conflict, he declared, careful study leads to the conclusion that this only *seems* to be the case. It disappears when the text is scrutinized with the more analytically learned eyes of the highly trained observer. When faith and reason clash, the Torah can often be seen to be speaking in allegory, he wrote. Clearly, he pointed out, there are statements in the Holy Book that can be refuted by proof and therefore must be interpreted in some other way. But its words must never be dismissed, for they were dictated by God to Moses and are therefore not only infallible but divine. With only this caveat, Maimonides was firmly convinced that Aristotelean thought could and should be incorporated into Jewish scripture—both Torah and Talmud—to the benefit of his people's theology and perhaps even to its benefit in the eyes of the non-Jewish world.

The object of this treatise is to enlighten a religious man who has been trained to believe in the truth of our holy Law, who conscientiously fulfills his moral and religious duties, and at the same time has been successful in his philosophical studies. Human reason has attracted him to abide within its sphere; and he finds it difficult to accept as correct the teaching based on a literal interpretation of the Law, and especially that which he himself or others derived from those homonymous, metaphorical, or hybrid expressions. Hence he is lost in perplexity and anxiety. If he be guided solely by reason, and renounce his previous views which are based on those expressions, he would consider that he had rejected the fundamental principles of the Law; and even if he retains the opinions which were derived from those expressions, and if, instead of following his reason, he abandons its guidance altogether, it would still appear that his religious convictions had suffered loss and injury. For then he would be left with those errors which give rise to fear and anxiety, constant grief and great perplexity.

Maimonides labored at the *Guide* for more than three years, not finishing it until 1190, when he was fifty-two years old, after recurrent bouts of illness had sapped much of his vigor. From the beginning, he recognized that he had set himself an overwhelming task. His attempt to minimize the conflict between faith and reason faltered in those sections where the disagreements proved insoluble despite every attempt to rationalize the differences. When such a situation was encountered, Maimonides generally dealt with it by taking the position that it was the philosophy or science that was in the wrong.

But not always. When objective evidence existed of rabbinical error, he did not hesitate to point it out. Commenting on certain mistakes made by the sages in estimating astronomic distance, for example, he pointed out that it was justified to correct them because their statements were based on the knowledge of their time rather than the incontrovertible sayings of the prophets.

> Do not ask of me to show that everything they [the Talmudic sages] have said concerning astronomic matters conforms to the way things really are. For at that time mathematics was imperfect. They did not speak about this as transmitters of the dictates of the prophets, but rather because in those times they were men of knowledge in these fields or because they had heard these dicta from the men of knowledge who lived in those times.

He then pointed out that when a fact or figure could actually be demonstrated to be erroneous—and the calculation of astronomical distances was an example—one should do so. This was a bold assertion, and one that had never before been made. But his position in such matters was firm. When the writings of the sages were contradicted by demonstrable facts, then "rabbinic statements should be regarded as individual opinions and not as halakha. Accordingly, they may be rejected."

The flavor of this statement should be tasted very carefully. Its author has disagreed with the Talmud on perfectly logical grounds, and has maintained—in fact has increased—its authority by correcting an obvious error. To Maimonides, the writing of the *Guide* was not so much an attempt to reconcile two different worldviews as to show that they were not only compatible but actually supportive of each other. From his earliest writings, he seems to have been imbued with the conviction that the logic and philosophies of the Greeks were not necessarily inconsistent with Holy Writ, so long as Holy Writ was interpreted at the intellectual level on which a mind highly trained in its complexities and true meaning was able to interpret it. Seeing through the parables and metaphorical allegories was difficult, and Maimonides' purpose was to guide his readers— those few so intelligent and well schooled that they could journey with him—toward the real truth of Jewish law, a truth that could in so many ways be sustained by the methods of the philosophers.

It must be recognized that the relationship between faith and reason was hardly a problem with which only Maimonides struggled, nor were its complexities and proposed solutions unique to his thought. Not only was his contemporary Averroës saying much the same thing of the Muslim scriptures, but the conciliation between faith and reason was occupying a very few of the best minds of the period. Avicenna had grappled with it in the early part of the eleventh century, as had the Jewish poet and philosopher of Andalusia, ibn Gabirol. In the century after Maimonides, it would engage the talents of such brilliant thinkers as Albertus Magnus and his student, Thomas Aquinas, both of whom found good reason to study the works of their rabbinic predecessor. It is hardly an exaggeration to point out that it was the major philosophical problem of the eleventh, twelfth, and thirteenth centuries. It has, of course, never left the arena of speculation; the reverberations of the words written by these Christian, Muslim, and Jewish masters can be heard to the present day.

For Maimonides, using the methods of the philosophers was a different thing than agreeing with them at every turn. The fact that he sometimes rejected their teachings because they could not in all instances be reconciled with his view of ultimate revealed truth did not lessen his conviction that the one could be used to strengthen the other. Of course, logic and faith have certain basic incompatibilities, he seems to have been saying, but they also have certain mutually reinforcing principles that only the elect are capable of perceiving. Because of his judgment that there is no need to simplify for the benefit of that elect, the *Guide* has proven over the centuries to be a hard nut to crack. It is filled with esoterica and mystifying commentary that have served as fodder for scholars ever since they were put down on paper. There is obviously more in its pages than meets the eye—

a great deal of the discussion and argument through the ages has been about just how *much* more. And a great deal, particularly in recent times, has concerned itself with yet another question: What was Maimonides really hiding within the abstruse sentences and between the seemingly impenetrable lines of his greatest book? There are those who believe he was more Greek than Jew.

And they can hardly be blamed. Here is a religious leader of the medieval period whose rigorous approach to truth was a powerful echo of his Hippocratic forebears and would resonate for centuries to come with his philosophical heirs. "A man should believe nothing," he wrote, "that is not attested (1) by rational proof, as in mathematical science, (2) by evidence of his senses, or (3) by authority of prophets or saints." The factor of authority would not be thrown off until well into the Enlightenment of the eighteenth century, but even in that, the standard of Maimonides is exquisitely high: It is "only prophets and saints" who are not to be questioned, and this could be taken to refer only to those so characterized by the text whose Pentateuch was written by the biblical Moses himself. This statement of the Rambam's is far more that of a rationalist thinker than of a man of unquestioning faith; considering the era in which he lived, it is indeed the statement of a thinker in the Aristotelean model.

Maimonides was aware that his undertaking in the *Guide* could only hope to approximate an idealized completion. But he also knew from his experience with the *Mishneh Torah* that he would be making himself the target not only of men with honest disagreements but also of those whose motives were far less objective.

I do not presume to think that this treatise settles every doubt in the minds of those who understand it, but I maintain that it settles the greater part of their difficulties. No intelligent man will require and expect that on introducing any subject I shall completely exhaust it; or that on commencing the exposition I shall fully explain its parts. Such a course could not be followed by a teacher in a *viva voce* exposition, much less by an author in writing a book, without becoming a target for every foolish conceited person to discharge the arrows of folly at him.

And that is precisely what happened. While many readers acclaimed the *Guide* (despite their limited understanding of its complexities), there were plenty of dissenters, among them some of the author's accustomed antagonists. The loud debates about the validity of the book continued long after the death of Maimonides, and they are heard in some quarters even today. Those who comprehend it only at face value (even this surface level of understanding is fraught with difficulties) and those who find esoteric meaning alike have joined a chorus of discussions, both resounding and muted, that will never be silent.

During the years when he was penning the letters to Joseph that would become the substance of the *Guide*, the burden of Moses's other work was gradually becoming greater and greater. As his international stature increased; as his medical practice grew; as his responsibilities to the sultan's court became more demanding; as the clamor for his counsel in the Egyptian Jewish community rose—he found himself inundated with demands on his time. He was frequently called upon to adjudicate points of the law and disputes, and the number of letters needing responsa was ever growing. He wrote many of them and the letters in his own hand, using the same kind of quill pen that he employed for his essays and treatises. A letter he wrote to Joseph shortly after this period describes his being too busy to study other than medical books except on the Sabbath, when he could find an opportunity to read in the Bible. In the same communication, he tells of the stature he has achieved as a physician: "And I hereby inform you that I have acquired very great renown in the practice of medicine among the great ones, such as the chief of judges and the emirs and the house of el Fadil and the other rulers of the land." And then, with obvious regret, he added, "And as for the people, I am exalted above them and they are unable to approach me." He was finally named *nagid* in 1187, restoring that office from its previous state of disgrace and at the same time adding another factor to his burden of work. He was now chief rabbi of the lands dominated by Saladin, chief judge of the Jews, chief of all philanthropies, and the administrative chief who appointed all community officials. Not only that, but 1187 was the same year in which he was made physician to Saladin's court.

The dispute with Samuel ibn Ali had been a constant source of distress for Maimonides throughout its long duration, but at least there was no overt attempt on his life, as occurred with another conflict in which he became involved at about this time. It will be recalled that he was indebted to a Muslim friend, Abul Arab ibn Moisha, for interceding in his behalf when the authorities in Fez were charging him with falsely claiming to be a convert to Islam. Whether or not he was actually arrested is uncertain, but it is known that he fell into the hands of the authorities and barely escaped the fate of his teacher, the distinguished Rabbi Judah ibn Shoshan, who was executed following a period of torture when he was discovered to be a pseudo-convert. At great personal risk, ibn Moisha had defended his young friend and assured his accusers that he was indeed a practicing Muslim. This courageous act on the part of a man convinced that he was justified in such a defense procured the release of Moses, which allowed him and the entire Maimon family to depart for Alexandria.

One can only imagine ibn Moisha's chagrin when he arrived on a business visit to Fustat in 1187 and discovered that the man he had risked so much to defend as a Muslim was now the leader of the Jewish community. Not only had his faith been betrayed, but so had his friendship. He denounced his old friend as a lapsed convert, a crime punishable by execution even though the offender was physician to the court of Saladin.

Because el Fadil placed high value on his newly appointed doctor, he arranged to become head of the tribunal before which Maimonides was brought for judgment. El Fadil was far more tolerant of other religions than most of the Muslim rulers, and he represented a sultan well known for his restraint in dealing with Christians and Jews. With characteristic liberality, he declared that Maimonides had not really converted to Islam and accordingly could not correctly be accused of lapsing from acquired faith. This enabled the accused's release and return to the freedom he had enjoyed until then.

It was in this same year, 1187, that Saladin won a great victory over the Christian forces and came into control of Jerusalem. Demonstrating the humanity for which he had become known, he forbade his soldiers to perpetrate the horrors to which the Crusaders had subjected the people of the city when they conquered it eighty-eight years earlier. And he also—some think at the request of Maimonides— invited all Jews to return to Palestine. It is part of the Maimonidean legend that the defeated Richard the Lionhearted sent a message asking Moses to come as his personal physician when he returned to England in 1192, and was refused. This was hardly the historical moment for any Jew to move willingly to a Christian country, especially in view of the tolerance that characterized the lands ruled by Saladin. In

England particularly, hatred was so intense that anti-Jewish riots occurred and many murders were committed only two years later, at the time of the Third Crusade.*

Shortly after Moses completed *The Guide for the Perplexed* in 1190, he began receiving requests from Jews in Christian countries that it be translated into Hebrew. Inundated with so many other responsibilities, he was unable to comply, but he was pleased a few years later when the rabbis of Provence asked him for a copy in its original Arabic and engaged a highly regarded scholar, Samuel ibn Tibbon, to do the work. Though there were by then two other translations, they had been done by men of lesser ability and were not completely satisfactory. Maimonides was especially pleased when he was informed that Samuel, whose father was also a well-known rabbi and translator, would undertake to provide a text that could be read by Jews everywhere. With his permission, the title of the book was to be translated as *Moreh Nevukhim*.

The two men began a correspondence, in which Samuel would write asking for advice about difficult passages. In one of his letters, Maimonides made some suggestions that can serve as a guide to translators everywhere.

---

*Although the story has traditionally been told this way, it is more likely that the Christian king whom Maimonides refused to serve was Amalric, and that this event occurred near the beginning of his career as a practicing physician. A text written by the Muslim biographer Ibn al-Quifti, a close friend of Joseph ibn Aknin, says of Maimonides, "The people used to read with him the sciences of the ancients—this was in the last years of the Fatimid rule in Egypt—and wished to give him employment among the

Whoever wishes to translate, and aims at rendering each word literally, and at the same time adheres slavishly to the order of the words and sentences in the original, will meet with much difficulty; his renderings will be faulty and untrustworthy. This is not the right method. The translator should first try to grasp the sense of the passage thoroughly and then state the author's intention with perfect clarity in the other language. This, however, cannot be done without changing the order of words, putting many words for one, or vice versa, and adding or taking away words, so that the subject may be perfectly intelligible in the language into which he translates.

Samuel generally followed this advice, but he was not the master of style that Maimonides had hoped he would be. Though his translation is said to be accurate, modern Hebrew scholars point out that it is rather dull and in places even more difficult to understand than the original. The cadence, rhythm, and subtlety that scholars find in the writings of the Rambam are not to be discovered in Samuel's *Moreh Nevukhim*.

---

physicians; they wished to send him to the Frankish king at Ascalon, because the latter had asked them for a physician, and so they chose him. But he refused to do this service and to join in this affair, and persisted in his refusal. When Nureddin became the master of Egypt, and the Fatimid rule was thrown down, el Fadil took him over and fixed for him an allowance. So he joined the other physicians."

At one point during the years of work, Samuel wrote to Maimonides asking for permission to visit him in Fustat. He received a response describing the enormity of the burden carried by the Rambam during the last years of his life, when his endurance, his health, and his very existence were daily threatened by the magnitude of his responsibilities. This letter is perhaps the most quoted passage in all of Maimonidean literature. It was written in 1199, while the sixty-one-year-old sage was recovering from a bout of the heart disease that plagued him. Though the general truth of the image sketched out here cannot be doubted, a modern reader should not be blamed for wondering whether a few of the details are so meticulously delineated because the writer was simply trying to discourage his correspondent from a visit that would only serve to further consume the hours of his day.

Now God knows that in order to write this to you I have escaped to a secluded spot, where people would not think to find me, sometimes leaning for support against a wall, sometimes lying down on account of my excessive weakness, for I have grown old and feeble.

With regard to your wish to come here to me, I cannot but say how greatly your visit would delight me, for I truly long to commune with you, and would anticipate our meeting with even greater joy than you. Yet I must advise you not to expose yourself to the perils of the voyage, for beyond seeing me, and my doing all I could to honor you, you would not derive any advantage from your visit. Do not expect to be able to confer with me on any scientific subject, for even one hour by day or night, for the following is my daily occupation. I dwell at Fustat and the Sultan [by then, the Sultan was Saladin's son, al Afdal; there is no evidence that Maimonides had ever met Saladin] resides at Cairo; these two places are two Sabbath days' journey [a mile and a half] distant from each other. My duties to the Sultan are very heavy. I am obliged to visit him every day, early in the morning; and when he or any of his children, or any of the inmates of his harem, are indisposed, I dare not quit Cairo, but must stay during the greater part of the day in the palace. It also frequently happens that one or two of the royal officers fall sick, and I must attend to their healing. Hence, as a rule, I repair to Cairo very early in the day, and if nothing unusual happens, I do not return to Fustat until the afternoon. Then I am almost dying with hunger. I find the antechamber filled with people, both Jews and Gentiles, nobles and common people, judges and bailiffs, friends and foes—a mixed multitude, who await the time of my return.

I dismount from my animal, wash my hands, go forth to my patients, and entreat them to bear with me while I partake of some slight refreshment, the only meal I take in the twenty-four hours. Then I attend to my patients and write prescriptions for their various ailments. Patients go in and out until nightfall, and sometimes even I solemnly assure you, until two hours and more into the night. I converse and prescribe for them while lying down from sheer fatigue, and when night falls, I am so exhausted that I can scarcely speak.

In consequence of this, no Israelite can have any private interview with me except on the Sabbath. On this day the whole congregation, or at least the majority of its members, come to me after the morning service, when I instruct them as to their proceedings during the whole week; we study together a little until noon, when they depart. Some of them return, and read with me after the afternoon service and until evening prayers. In this manner I spend that day. I have here related to you only a part of what you would see if you were to visit me. Now, when you have completed for our brethren the translation you have commenced, I beg that you will come to me but not with the hope of deriving any advantage from your visit as regards your studies; for my time is, as I have shown you, excessively occupied.

As if all of this were not enough, Maimonides produced some ten small books on medicine during perhaps the last dozen years of his life. The one generally thought to be first,

*On Sexual Intercourse*, seems to have been written at the behest of Saladin's nephew, Al Muzaffar Umar ibn Nur ad Din, who was the sultan of Hamah in Syria. The sultan was a very thin man, almost to the point of emaciation, but he had refused to take the advice given him by Maimonides, which was to severely restrict his profligate sexual activities among the young women in his harem and elsewhere. When he found himself faced with a situation that Maimonides describes as "the increase of a large number of concubines," he asked that a manual be written for him so that he might make the most of his good fortune without endangering his health.

In producing such a book, Maimonides was following a well-worn path in Arabic literature. There had long existed a genre of this kind, ranging along a spectrum from the strictly clinical to marital manuals to texts that were flagrantly salacious, all of them purporting to help with the wide variety of problems associated with sexual activity. The book written by Maimonides describes the proper use of herbal agents, aphrodisiac and anaphrodisiac foods, and manual activities such as massage of the coccyx, anal sphincter, and upper thighs. The wine made from a plant called oxtongue is recommended because it "greatly increases the joy of sexual intercourse."

Maimonides went on to write a series of monographs on medicine, added work that only served to exhaust him further. As always, there were new projects on the horizon:

Having been criticized for omitting references in the *Mishneh Torah*, he was now determined to correct what he considered an error; there were the translations of his works into Hebrew to supervise; he had long contemplated writing a book on the Jerusalem Talmud; there were other treatises he hoped to produce. But the strength in his aging, careworn body was being sapped with each passing day. Saladin died in 1193, and five years later, the great sultan's profligate son, al Afdal, became ruler and appointed Maimonides chief physician to the court. But by the time al Afdal lost the throne, within two years of assuming it, that chief physician had become too sick and debilitated to travel to Cairo.

And yet, the writing of letters and responsa did not end. Although he needed his nephew to act as his scribe, Maimonides continued to work until the last day of his life. He died on December 13, 1204 (in the Jewish calendar, 20 Tevet 4965), while dictating the last chapter of a book of his aphorisms. He was sixty-six years old. The Jewish community of Egypt declared three days of mourning for him, to be spent in prayer and contemplation. Many Muslims joined in their grief.

Even in death, the making of myths continued to surround the great rabbi. One of them is the fanciful tale that his coffin was placed on the back of a donkey, which was then allowed to wander where it would, finally coming to a stop in Tiberias. But the far more common version tells of the funeral procession that was taking his body to that city—where he had asked to be buried—being attacked by a band of Bedouins who tried to cast the coffin into the sea. But it proved to be so inexplicably heavy that they became convinced that it must contain the remains of a holy man whom they should honor. Joining the procession, they accompanied the mourners to the final resting place of Moses, the greatest Jewish sage since Moses.

# Maimonides, Physician

> Although from my boyhood the Torah was be-
> trothed to me and continued to hold my heart as
> the wife of my youth, strange women whom I first
> took into my house as her handmaids became her
> rivals and absorb a portion of my time.
>
> *Letter of Moses Maimonides to*
> *Jonathan of Lunel, France, 1195*

I bn Abi Usaybi'a, a Muslim physician living in Syria in the
thirteenth century, said of Moses Maimonides that he had
been "unique in his time in the theory and practice of medicine." That very short statement embodies a historical
assessment that deserves some analysis, in order to deter-
mine whether the conventionally accepted thesis that the
Rambam's medical stature—in his time and since—does, in
fact, deserve to be called towering. Indeed, just how unique
a doctor and medical innovator was he?

Such an analysis most properly begins with "his time."

What was the contemporary state of "the theory and practice of medicine" in the twelfth century, and how was it affected by Moses's teachings and his daily round of patient care? Did he add to the general sum of knowledge? Did he make any new discoveries? At his death, were the "theory and practice" of medicine of "the time" significantly different than they might have been had he never lived? And most important for posterity, did he leave a heritage that succeeding generations of physicians could look to as a model of the grand tradition of their art and science?

The era in which Maimonides lived was a period during which medicine, like so much else, may be said to have been in a state best described as a holding pattern. Though recent historical scholarship has shown that the word *medieval* has been much misused as a synonym for intellectually stagnant, even the most avid and rectifying apologists for those centuries must concede that there nevertheless do remain certain areas in which the term *Dark Ages* has some real meaning. Medicine is one of them.

In an age when the voice of authority was the most significant influence in determining belief, philosophy, and the understanding of nature, the persisting ghost of a single man loomed over medical thought like an overpowering colossus. That man was the second-century C.E. Greek physician Galen of Pergamon. Building on the teachings of the school of Hippocrates, Galen codified a medicine based on the notion of the balance of four liquids, called humors, within the body of each individual. A dearth or overabundance of any of them—blood, yellow bile, black bile, or phlegm—was said by him to be the cause of disease, which was to be treated by restoring the balance through purgatives, enemas, bloodletting, and similar stratagems. But before embarking on such interventions, more moderate means were to be employed, such as changes in diet and the prescribing of complex mixtures of certain botanical preparations, often those resulting in the purging of a surfeit of one or another humor. The primitive surgery of the time was used only for appropriate indications, such as injuries, infections of the extremities, and tumors on the surface of the body.

During his lifetime, Galen was a showman of medical practice and experimentation. Not only did he foster the preexisting Hippocratic teachings about humors and much else, but he went far beyond them, proclaiming himself the sole intellectual heir to the ancient Father of Medicine. He conducted public lectures, often including dramatic experiments on living animals, demonstrating repeatedly before crowds of enthusiastic onlookers certain physiological and anatomical characteristics of the mammalian body previously unknown. He wrote profusely and grandiloquently of his research and of the proper ways to treat disease, insisting that only his methods were to be followed, as he described them in a corpus of self-glorifying literature so vast that, when collected and translated into German in the early nineteenth century, it filled the pages of twenty-two thick octavo volumes.

Not only was Galen the leading physician of his time and personal doctor to the emperor Marcus Aurelius, but he did not hesitate to declare himself the everlasting mahatma of medicine. "Whoever seeks fame by deeds, not alone by learned speech," he wrote for the benefit of centuries of physicians who would follow him, "need only become familiar, at small cost of trouble, with all that I have achieved by active research during the course of my entire life." To Galen and to his many generations of acolytes, he had discovered all that needed to be known of the human body, its diseases, and their treatment; his was a complete system of medicine, requiring no future modifications. And he was believed. No one before him had advanced medical knowledge as much as he, and no one had so perfectly assured his own sainthood. Galen left a body of theory and a form of writ considered so conclusive that it was the unchallenged canon of medicine for almost fifteen hundred years.

By the fourth century C.E., the power of Rome had given way to the Eastern Empire whose capital was Constantinople. The energies of that empire, deeply invested in wars, conflicts, and intrigues so tortuous that the term *byzantine* would later enter our vocabulary, were hardly directed to science, whose progress virtually stopped in all the Christian lands, including those of western Europe. But when the Muslim nation exploded out of the Arabian peninsula in the eighth century, it carried with it a contagious zest for learning that served as the basis for a brilliantly exciting new culture, spreading rapidly through the expanding territories controlled by the conquerors. It might be said that, unlike Christianity, the Islamic nation *began* its existence with a renaissance.

One of the most influential manifestations of the Muslim eagerness for knowledge was the translation into Arabic of the ancient Greek scientific texts. Euclid, Ptolemy, and especially Aristotle became lodestars to the Islamic thinkers. In medicine, the writings of the Hippocratic authors and of Galen formed the basis of the new Arabic medicine, which was informed almost exclusively by their writings, widely disseminated because they were the ultimate medical texts of the Greco-Roman period. Arabic physicians had access to these giants not by reading the original Greek but via commentaries on translations made in the late eighth and early ninth centuries by Jewish, Syrian Christian, and Zoroastrian Persian scholars. At first, the scribes worked from original Greek manuscripts, but as these became more difficult to find, they did their translating from Latin versions that had been made by Byzantine scholars in the fourth, fifth, and sixth centuries. Another major source was the works of the seventh-century scholar Paul of Aegina, whose *Seven Books* interpreting the two ancient masters were translated from Latin into Arabic two hundred years after they were written and became—though reinterpreted, edited, and modestly expanded—one of the foundation stones of medicine during the entire period when Arabic-speaking physicians were at the height of their repute.

Using these various translations and redactions, widely read books were produced by a small group of Byzantine, Jewish, or Muslim physicians who commented on them and made their own small additions, not infrequently shot through with the errors characteristic of the revisionist. Even the great Islamic innovators of the period who read the Greek authors in their original eighth- and ninth-century translations were not immune to a tendency to misinterpret their ideas or rehash them uncritically. The gigantic tome written in the eleventh century by the most highly praised of the Islamic physicians, Abu Ali al-Hussein ibn Abdallah ibn Sina, or, as he became known in the West, Avicenna, was the most authoritative work of the period, and yet much of it, like so many other canonical Arabic medical writings, was a rehash of Galen, more than occasionally misunderstood. Not only that, but Avicenna's book valued logic and reasoning over clinical experience, turning the reader away from the personal observation that is the most direct path to real comprehension of disease and therapy.

In all of these ways Arabic books became the repository of Greek medicine, and of science in general. Obviously, these texts were more accurate when they came directly from the original Greek than by the circuitous route of Latin and the redaction that the Byzantine and other authors frequently inserted, not to mention the increased possibility of error caused by doubling or further multiplying the number of translations. While Maimonides was thoroughly familiar

with the works of his most eminent Arabic predecessors—
and sometimes quoted them in his own medical writings—
he seems to have followed a less circuitous route than did
most of them. He studied the texts of antiquity in Arabic
translation directly from the original Greek, and did not rely
on the later commentators and revisionists to help him.

The system by which Muslim and Jewish physicians writing in Arabic commented on translations of the ancient
authorities worked both ways. Because the Greek medical
literature became the subject of commentary and even edit-
ing by Arabic-speaking physicians, the contemporary doctors were able to insert their own particularistic viewpoints
into the text and into the theoretics of healing. It is thus
a great historical process that is here being described, in
which Muslim and Jewish thinking became infused into
the ancient Greek precepts. All of the major figures of the
Arabic period—Haly Abbas, Rhazes, Avicenna, Albucasis,
Avenzoar, Averroës, and the Jewish writer Isaac Judaeus—
were, in fact, interpreters of Galen. The basis of their
stature in history does not consist of having made new contributions to medical knowledge, but of the ways in which
their fresh perspectives on the ancient teachings were useful
to the physicians of their time and later. This is precisely
how historians view the contributions of Maimonides.

In other words, Maimonides did not discover anything
new. He was not a researcher, nor did he make original
clinical contributions. He was, like so many of the eminent
medical leaders of the period, a commentator on the art of

medicine as it had been handed down to him by Hippocrates and especially by Galen, basing the commentary on his worldview and the experiences he had had when caring for his many thousands of patients. And his worldview embraced not only the clinical treatment of disease, but its psychological and spiritual aspects, as well as the ethical concerns that arose from his uniquely Jewish perspective and his uniquely compassionate nature.

Maimonides came upon the medical scene at a time when little was known of the anatomy of the human body or the functioning of its various internal parts. Disease was seen as a generalized disorder of the entire patient, and not as it is today: a malfunctioning of individual organs and cells or their components. It was thought to be characterized by departures from equilibrium—such as imbalances of the four humors—that might be caused by any of a variety of mechanisms, all of which involved the totality of the organism and all of which were to be treated by restoring the balance. In such a system of medicine, knowing details of anatomy or the physiology of organs or tissues served no useful purpose, and such studies were not pursued beyond bare essentials. Moreover, the time-honored Greek aversion—amounting to revulsion—at handling the dead body more than was absolutely necessary had given rise to severe restrictions on the possibility of dissection. Though the Hippocratic teachings had established the principle that no supernatural forces were to be considered in either the causation or the treatment of illness, physicians and especially the laity nevertheless not infrequently invoked the role of God in healing, as an adjunct to medical therapies.

As noted earlier, those therapies consisted largely of changes in diet or daily habits, and the use of drugs that were composed of various botanical and sometimes mineral or animal products. A given prescription might include as many as ten or more such ingredients, after the fashion of Galen, who was so fond of multiply mixed compoundings that they had become known as galenicals. Few of these herbal preparations, if tested by twenty-first-century means, could be shown to have any effect at all. The reason for a particular herbal product's use was more mystical than real, being based on long-standing notions of efficacy attributed to such qualities as color, shape, and centuries of wishful thinking. Like the humors, the role of these therapies was theoretical and based on certain traditions handed down from generation to generation of physicians, often originating with Galen himself.

To become a doctor in the Middle Ages, one studied Galen's writings and those attributed to Hippocrates translated into either Arabic or Latin, depending on one's country of origin. Many aspiring physicians in the Muslim lands read the ancients only as interpreted and amended by the luminaries of contemporary medicine, most of whom were Persian or Spanish born, and sometimes Jewish, though they all wrote in Arabic. It was helpful to apprentice oneself to a physician, but only in order to see how colleagues applied the Galenic principles to patients in actual practice. Those thought to be the best doctors were those who best knew how to understand Galen and to use his methods for achieving cure. Medical progress, as we understand it today in the form of a constantly expanding corpus of knowledge about the body and the processes of disease—and in the philosophy that there is still a great deal to be discovered—had been at a standstill since the death of the immortal Greek in 201 C.E. It would remain that way until the sixteenth century. Looking back with a present-day eye on the medicine of the medieval period, one cannot escape the judgment that patients got better or worse depending far less on the treatment than on the natural history of their disease.

It is difficult to know precisely how Maimonides acquired his medical knowledge. Almost certainly, its origins lay in the general process of educating an intellectually well-rounded young man of the time, one whose family valued all forms of learning. The influence was both Greek and Jewish. To be fully educated required the study of mathematics, astronomy, ancient philosophy, botany, and medicine, all of them the heritage of Greek thought. And the Rambam's religious belief required that he see health as a precondition of understanding God. "A man should aim to maintain physical health and vigor," he wrote in Book I of the *Mishneh Torah*, "in order that his soul may be upright, in a condition to know God." To this statement of faith he then added a statement of secular philosophy: "For it is impossible for one to understand sciences and meditate upon them, when he is hungry or sick." In these two sentences, written one after the other, can be seen an epitome of the mind of the great sage. Taken together, they represent the grand themes that run through so much of the Maimonidean writings about medicine and about the pursuit of scientific and philosophic learning. Side by side, united by the shared necessity for good health, can be seen the two motives that guided his life: to comprehend the ways of God, and to comprehend the ways of man and the natural universe. The key to both was relentless study. Far less than many have thought, declared Maimonides, were these two goals in conflict with each other.

And so, it is probable that Moses began the study of Galen and Hippocrates during his childhood. In the process of trying to continue his education during the family's unsettled time in eastern Spain, he almost certainly continued to pore over whatever texts might fortuitously come into his hands. With his extraordinary ability to remember so much of what he read, he must have been quite familiar with the Greek authors by the time he arrived in Morocco. There are hints in his writings that he may have worked with several physicians in Fez, which would have given him some experience in the actual treatment of patients. However, it is at least equally probable that Maimonides had never had clinical instruction in medicine prior to beginning his own practice in Fustat. Not only was this a route sometimes taken by aspiring doctors, but some of the leading Muslim physicians believed the study of books to be sufficient unto itself, as adequate preparation for the care of patients. From pages found in the *Genizah*, it is known that the Arabic term describing the contemporary method of medical education was *quara'a 'ala'a*, whose literal meaning is "to read something with someone." Either way—exclusively by study, or with the addition of some clinical experience—we can be sure that, like the rest of his unceasing quest for knowledge, his study of medical texts continued unabated. Considering his masterful knowledge of other branches of learning, the conclusion cannot be escaped that, by the time of his arrival in Fustat, Maimonides had become an authority on both the Greek medical writers and the Muslim and Jewish authors of his own era. Based on the treatises to which he made reference, it is known—as stated earlier—that he read the Greeks in Arabic translations made directly from the originals, thus avoiding the possibility of additional error introduced by the Greek-to-Latin-to-Arabic route.

Without such a thorough and comprehensive understanding of the ancient and contemporary authors, Maimonides could not have produced the ten works that constitute his medical legacy. But no matter the depth of his textual knowledge, it was his vast experience as a practicing physician that leavened his perceptions and ultimately determined the quality of his texts. Though they are for the most part a distillation of authors past and contemporary, the reader senses that this is no distanced bookworm-doctor writing; it is a wise and skillful bedside clinician, who knew that a deep empathy could lead patients toward healthy forms of behavior in an era when little else of value was available. Even as he repeated the advice he culled from the literature, there is a tone of concern in these books that reflects all that is present as a suffusion throughout the *Commentary on the Mishnah*, the *Mishneh Torah*, and the extant letters. Medical references are scattered throughout these Jewish writings, primarily to preventive methods and emotional health, sometimes referred to as "diseases of the soul." The two topics are dealt with extensively in the *Mishneh Torah*, which includes a section specifically titled just that: "Diseases of the Soul."

Maimonides wrote all of his medical books in Arabic, with Arabic lettering. A review of their contents reveals very much what might be expected from a medical writer of the time, but there are just enough distinctly Maimonidean touches to verify at least an innovation of approach if not of discovery, particularly in the realm of psychological aspects in illness. This makes itself more evident in some of the ten treatises than in others.

At five hundred pages in a recent translation, the largest—and certainly the most important—of the books is the one known in Hebrew as *Pirkei Moshe* and in English as *The Medical Aphorisms of Moses*, the work for which he became best known in Christian Europe. Despite its title, the volume consists mostly of a compilation from the works of Galen and several other Greek authors on the body in health and disease, as well as sections from their texts dealing with bleeding, purging, puking, surgery, other therapies, and the diseases of women. Following the standard form of Arabic medical literature, the book is subdivided into twenty-five discourses on about fifteen hundred aphorisms, with little that is new. But the last discourse is, in fact, a departure from the approach of any but a few previous commentators. Prior to the appearance of this section, only a handful of writers (most prominent among them being Avenzoar of Cordoba, a generation earlier) had dared to question Galen, either in issues of fact or of perspective. Not only does Maimonides—despite his admiration for his vaunted predecessor—here point out forty errors and contradictions in the Galenic writings, but he attacks the presumptuousness of the ancient Greek for making statements about matters that he does not fully understand, arising out of arrogant presumption. Galen "considers himself more perfect than he really is," writes Maimonides in one of the aphorisms.

It is in the *Aphorisms* that Maimonides elucidates his conviction about the nature of evidence, an underlying theme in the development of medical knowledge since the time of Hippocrates and even today. Elsewhere he had written that the only nonobjective criterion for belief is "the authority of prophets and saints." And now, in the most detailed of his medical writings, he made frontal assault on the entire edifice of authority—most particularly Galen's—in a statement so bold for its time as to represent virtual heresy in contemporary medical teachings, where the ancient Greek was considered to be both a prophet and a secular saint of medicine. The *Aphorisms* of Maimonides could only have been written by a physician of such vast personal bedside experience that he understood the pragmatic necessity of verifying everything for himself; and it could only have been written by a physician of such vast personal self-assurance that he dared to question the oracle.

If anyone declares to you that he has actual proof from his own experiences, of something which he requires for the confirmation of his theory, even though he be considered a man of great authority, truthfulness, earnest words and morality, yet just because he is anxious for you to believe his theory, you should hesitate. Do not allow your mind to be swayed by the "novelties" which he tells you, but look well into his theory and his belief, just as you should do concerning the things which he declares that he has seen; look into the matter without letting yourself be easily persuaded. And this is true whether the person is notable or one of the people. For a strong will may lead a man to speak erringly—especially in disputation. I offer this in order to awaken your interest in the statements of that wise man, that prince, Galen.

In the same six-paragraph passage, Maimonides makes a statement echoing his *Commentary on the Mishnah* and other works, demonstrating his characteristic attention to psychological and spiritual aspects of illness: "The soul can be healthy or diseased, just as the body is either healthy or diseased." This simple declaration is a foundation stone of Maimonidean medicine and a recurrent theme in many of his writings.

It is significant that Maimonides makes a point in this book of vigorously defending Aristotle in those situations where Galen disagrees with him, whether about the human body or any concept of philosophy. Moreover, he is frankly harsh when the ancient physician decries some principle of religion that his Greek mind finds impossible to believe, going so far as to refer to him as "this falsifying and inexact Galen, extremely ignorant of most things of which he speaks except in the art of medicine."

This calling of Galen to account was rare at the time, and would be rare for another four centuries, until 1543, when the twenty-eight-year-old anatomist Andreas Vesalius of Brussels publicly and forcefully demonstrated some two hundred errors he had discovered in Galenic anatomy, including the revelation that one of the most significant structures on which his theory of the human psyche was based did not exist. Even this did not end the Galenic hegemony, which was destined to endure for almost three more centuries, slowly petering out before being destroyed completely. But Maimonides was among the first to point to the feet of clay that would eventually crumble sufficiently to bring down the entire icon. When the Arabic scientific literature was later translated into Latin—a process that reached its peak in the thirteenth century—the Rambam's works entered the canon of Western medicine and remained there for centuries: In the ninety years between 1489 and 1579, for example, no fewer than five Latin editions of *The Medical Aphorisms of Moses* were published in Europe.

Maimonides wrote two other books based directly on the work of Greek eminences. One, *The Extracts*, was a series of selections from Galen intended for the students he frequently taught, without any essential change in the text. The other was in a genre that many other Arab medical writers had already employed: He wrote comments on the most famous work attributed to Hippocrates, his *Aphorisms*. Although Maimonides does in general follow the text of a commentary on the same material made by Galen, he occasionally departs from it to criticize some of the statements of the Father of Medicine as being obscure, useless, or even false. Any twenty-first-century physician reading the Greek text would agree with him. For example, in response to the Hippocratic aphorism stating that a boy is born from the right ovary and a girl from the left, Maimonides wryly comments that "a man would have to be either a prophet or a genius to know this." Unlike the large tome based on Galen, which had editions in a number of European languages, this book was translated only into Hebrew.

The other seven books of Maimonides—described fully in the appendix of this volume—deal with clinical matters. But each of them is nevertheless a highly personal treatise, leavened with the concern of a dedicated doctor for the well-being not only of his patients' bodies but of their spirits. It was with good reason that the thirteenth-century poet and scholar al Said ibn Sina al-Mulk would characterize this healer who in his medical writings customarily introduces himself as "the Israelite from Cordoba" by pointing out that Galen might heal the body but Maimonides also healed the mind:

Galen's art heals only the body,
But abu-Imran's the body and the soul.
His knowledge made him the physician of the
    century.
His wisdom could cure the disease of ignorance.
If the moon would submit to his art,
He would deliver her from her spots at the time of the
    full moon,
Would relieve her of her monthly ailments.

What is to be made of the ten medical books of Maimonides, and, far more important, of their author? It must be reiterated that he was first and foremost a physician of his time. The only novelty in his work was the attention he paid—spread throughout but most particularly in his books *Discourse on the Explanation of Fits* and *On the Regulation of Health*—to the emotional life of his patients and his proposition that mental states influence disease. But even that was not truly original, except that he stressed it so much more than most other authors who had previously written about these factors that it is remembered by historians as a hallmark of his approach to disease. And in that stressing, his heritage was of significance to the many physicians who would read his works over the centuries. No aspect of medieval medicine was changed by it or by anything else he wrote, so in that sense his contribution to progress must be admitted to have been minimal. Even the fact of his criticizing Galen and Hippocrates was not unique.

And yet, when historians enumerate the medical luminaries of the Middle Ages, his name is more likely than not to be among them. Along with Rhazes, Haly Abbas, Avicenna, Albucasis, and Averroës, one usually finds Maimonides, and it is not difficult to understand why. The fact is that none of them did much more than comment and somewhat enlarge on the Galenic and Hippocratic literature, and the Rambam was not an exception.

Nor was the Rambam an exception in his emphasis on healthy living as the best means of preventing sickness. Like his Muslim colleagues, he was aware that he served his patients well by warning them, as he does in *The Guide for the Perplexed*, that "only one in a thousand persons dies a natural death [by which he almost certainly meant a death of old age]; the rest die early because of ignorant or aberrant behavior."

But one does have the sense that the writings of Maimonides were particularly useful to a physician who was seeking a clearly organized, accessible text written in so practical a way that it could be followed like a manual of patient care. In thinking about these things, one cannot but remember the Rambam's stated reasons for writing the *Mishneh Torah*—to make holy writ available in a form comprehensible and pervious to anyone who was reasonably capable of reading it; to provide an exposition that made it unnecessary to plow one's way through the sources on which it was based; to stimulate on the part of appropriately qualified persons the desire for further study of the Torah and Talmud. For Torah and Talmud, here read the Hippocratic and Galenic corpuses as well as those of his Arabic predecessors, such as Avicenna. These were, by and large, complex and ponderous books, difficult to read and retain in the mind. Fielding Garrison, the eminent early-twentieth-century historian of medicine, famously said of Avicenna's encyclopedic *Canon* that it was a "gigantic tome . . . , a huge unwieldy storehouse of learning." Two centuries earlier, the renowned physiologist Albrecht von Haller of Göttingen, who was also highly regarded as a historian of medicine, called the *Canon* a "methodic inanity." Though there were notable exceptions, the Arabic writings in general presented an imposing challenge for a student or practicing physician attempting to learn medicine or solve a clinical problem at the bedside. How much easier it must have been for the average Arabic or Jewish physician of the twelfth or thirteenth century to sit down with one of the small books of Maimonides and learn all that he needed to know. Of the several aspects of the Rambam's genius, the one that was surely most appreciated by readers in his time and later was his extraordinary ability to separate wheat from chaff and to collect, classify, and correlate needed information into a helpful, compact, and easily remembered whole.

To accomplish this required the vast knowledge that was a product of Maimonides' extraordinary memory and his ability to see all-embracing themes through the dense haze of minutiae and tedious detail. The greatest of his strengths was the quality that might be called the "synthesizing mind," that which enabled him to perceive parallels, connections, patterns, and unities in widely disparate masses of information and experience, and then to interpret and organize them into a meaningful, comprehensive, and apprehensible whole, while maintaining the virtue of conciseness. In doing this, he took material already in existence, imbued it with his own insights and perspectives, and made of it something new, achieving a creative synthesis that characterized his genius not only in medicine but in religious thought as well.

Accustomed to writing responsa on the basis of which major decisions were made in Jewish communities throughout the Muslim and Christian worlds (about half of his medical writings were, in fact, in the nature of responsa), Maimonides knew how to address specific important issues in a way that digested and clarified them while adjudicating differences of opinion with a voice of authority. He did this in a literate, attractive style that was not only easy to read but easy to remember as well. These are qualities with which few doctors have ever been gifted, whether they lived in the Middle Ages or live today.

Some estimate of Maimonides' continuing influence derives from the fact that most of his medical writings were translated into Latin as well as Hebrew, and in edition after edition. Not only were there the many editions of the *Aphorisms*, for example, but the book's active use by physicians can be traced as late as the middle of the seventeenth century.

And finally, there is the characteristic of Maimonidean writings that has been cherished right up to the present time, and will remain the hallmark of his lasting contribution. By this I mean the ethical principia that suffuses every product of his pen, whether it be a religious tractate such as the *Commentary on the Mishnah*, the *Mishneh Torah*, or the responsa; a more philosophical one like the *Guide;* a personal one like the archive of letters; or a seemingly pragmatic and secular one like a medical text. Though the underlying basis of his ethics is religious, its moral purpose is universal and permeated with the sense of obligation to the sick that must be the highest motivation of any healer. "Medical practice," he wrote, "is not knitting and weaving and the labor of the hands, but it must be inspired with soul and be filled with understanding." The keen powers of observation and the accurate clinical knowledge that he exemplified and taught were meant to be part of something much higher and more inclusive, an entire ethical formulation at the center of which is the patient. As his numerous biographers have pointed out again and again, he brought his entire worldview to medical practice: Ethics, philosophy, religion, and healing were to him a unity. Every patient and indeed every person he encountered was an individual within an ordered world, one whose intellectual and religious stability came from God and whose highest purpose was to know God. To that universal end, health is necessary, for only through health of mind and body is it possible to comprehend God's creations. And it is through study of God's creations that one can best approach an understanding of God. Thus, all knowledge and all ethics and all religion must be brought together with the aim of forming an integrated whole. In the *Mishneh Torah*, he wrote:

> Since, when the body is healthy and sound one directs oneself toward the ways of the Lord—it being impossible to understand or know anything of the knowledge of the Creator when one is sick—it is obligatory on man to avoid things which are detrimental to the body and seek out things which fortify it.

So much for Maimonides as a medical thinker. To evaluate him as a healer of individual patients is quite another matter, about which we have only circumstantial evidence and a few comments by men who wrote at the time or soon after. The scant number of such witnesses say that he was gifted and very highly skilled. He brought the entirety of his ethical and religious principia—not to mention that incomparable command of the literature and his keen perceptions as an observer—to the care of every patient, whether princely or poor.

But to say that the medical theory of Maimonides was based on his religious beliefs is not to say that his theology influenced either his notions of disease causation or of treatment. Quite the opposite; and in this he was like the Hippocratic physicians of old. Although they were devoutly committed to the supremacy of the gods, one of the singular defining characteristics of their contribution to medicine was its separation of the divine from the actual care of the sick. They introduced the notion that all disease has natural causes and must be treated with natural measures. The Hippocratic Oath is sworn "by Apollo the physician and Aesculapius, Hygeia and Panacea and all the gods and goddesses," but its contents—and indeed the entire Hippocratic corpus of diagnostic, therapeutic, and ethical writings—deal with the practical issues of patient care and medical education, as though those gods and goddesses did not exist. To them and to Maimonides, the physician's skills may have been God-given, but they were to be applied independently of any possible direct divine intervention. It is not prayer that one should rely on when sick, he argued, but medical aid; the means of curing disease are provided by God, but "He has given wise and skillful men the knowledge of how to prepare and how to apply them." It is to these wise and skillful physicians that one should turn when disease strikes.

Although this philosophy was hardly unique to Maimonides—it was a virtually universal theme of Jewish and Muslim medicine—the leaders of the medieval Christian church did not commonly share it. As noted in the first chapter of this book, ecclesiastical leaders in general promulgated the notion that individuals become sick for supernatural reasons, and therapies must accordingly come from on high rather than from doctors. In 1215, the Fourth Lateran Council decreed that physicians must not treat patients without the participation of clergy, under threat of excommunication (this, incidentally, was the council that declared that Jews must wear distinctive dress). And this state of affairs did not end with the medieval period. As late as the middle of the sixteenth century, Pope Pius V—that zealous persecutor of heretics, backsliders, and Jews—reinforced the decree and strengthened it, in part by ordering that a physician's treatment must be discontinued if, at the end of three days, the patient has not confessed to a priest, because, in his words, "bodily infirmity frequently arises from sin." That statement embodied the centuries-long tradition of the Church and, at least in part, explains why so many rulers and members of prominent families customarily sought medical counsel from Muslim and especially Jewish doctors.

But even Maimonides was not averse to employing a bit of clinical sleight of hand—and even superstition—when he thought it might benefit a patient. By all accounts, his notion of medicine as an art extended to the use of artfulness when he believed it to be necessary. Any thoughtful physician of the time, whether Muslim, Jewish, or Christian, had to have known that the value of much of the contemporary pharmacopeia lay in its placebo effect: If it worked at all, it was only because the patient (and perhaps the physician as well) believed that it would. Ethical principia or not, Maimonides was not above the sly trickery to which physicians have always resorted when dealing with the occasional patient for whom clinical judgment may indicate that it might be a measure of last resort. But for the Rambam, a doctor committed to the thesis of the mind's effect on the body, it was permissible to discard even the most cherished of medical convictions in the interest of a patient's psychological needs. An example is his attitude toward the therapeutic use of amulets and charms.

Since earliest times, amulets and charms were used to treat disease, sometimes along with incantations and prayer-like formulas written to enhance their efficacy. These were meant to function as a form of magic, and Maimonides railed against them in his teaching and writing as he did against any form of sorcery in treatment. Though God-directed prayers may be said for the sick, he believed, therapy must proceed along the outlines taught in medical treatises and verified at the bedside. The notion of working miracles by use of necromancy was anathema to his code. In the *Guide*, for example, he denounces as delusion the use of such mystical methods to purify a patient of illness and argues that they should not be sanctioned. And yet this pragmatic physician would in rare instances violate his own dictum—when the disease was severe and he had little else to offer. A concession to popular superstition was permissible under such circumstances, he wrote, "lest the mind of the patient be too greatly disturbed." To Maimonides, such an occasional subterfuge testified to the skill of the hands using it.

The circumstantial evidence of the skill of his own hands

was that he had an enormous practice; was chosen to be a high-ranking physician to the courts of rulers; and is shown in his medical, philosophical, and religious writing, as well as in the recorded details of his life, to have been a man of exceptional compassion, gentleness, and ethical principles. Since we know of his encyclopedic knowledge from reading his texts on medical practice, we can only conclude that he possessed the qualities to justify the luminous reputation as a clinician that he has carried through the ages.

Patients from every walk of life so clamored for this renowned doctor's services that he was frequently near exhaustion during his last decade. Except for the *Glossary of Drug Names*, all of the medical books were written during this time, even as his ever-enlarging practice grew out of control. Virtually every biography of his life contains somewhere in it the text of the letter he wrote to Samuel ibn Tibbon, because it describes the exhaustion to which his lifetime of relentless labor had left him prey.

The letter tells much more than Maimonides intended. Since the earliest glimmerings of Hippocratic medicine, no characteristic has so distinguished the ethical doctrines of the medical profession as the notion of obligation. Whatever motives of beneficence or religious commitment—or even scientific enthusiasm—may catalyze the healing instincts of Western-trained doctors, it is the conviction that the acceptance of a medical degree brings with it an obligation to individuals and to the greater society that is ultimately the most profound charge that they must accept. Medicine is not a profession for the summer soldier or the sunshine patriot. It is a calling and, as such, transcends the mere requirements of a career. It does not put itself to sleep for the night nor does it wander off into the realms of pleasure, so long as there is someone sick who has a need that can be fulfilled in no other way than by this particular doctor or a designated colleague. This is the essence not only of the social contract that the profession—the calling—has with humankind in general, but the moral contract that every physician worthy of the name has with himself or herself. Maimonides' oft-quoted letter is a testament to that contract, as it is being fulfilled by a doctor who is meticulously aware of what he is, what he means to his patients, and what he must do. Some might argue that the letter to ibn Tibbon describes a form of personal sacrifice beyond the call of such a sense of duty. Maimonides, from all we know of him, would at first perhaps not have comprehended that such an objection could so much as be raised. But he would soon have a response to it, a response no doubt embodied in the words of the famed prayer attributed to him, in which he attests to having been chosen by God "to watch over the life and health of your creatures." Whether the physician of today believes himself or herself to have been called by God or to have been self-chosen, the obligation is the same. There is no turning back from it.

To Jews, the Rambam has always been the compleat physician; in recent centuries, the well-known Prayer of Maimonides has become the testament of the ideal—and idealized—healer. It has rivaled the Hippocratic Oath as the statement by which a young physician pledges fealty to his art, his principles, and the trust of his patients. Unfortunately, it is also like the Hippocratic Oath in that it was not written by its putative author.

The so-called Prayer of Maimonides first appeared in the new German journal *Deutsches Museum* in 1783, bearing the description, "Daily prayer of a physician before he visits his patients: from the Hebrew manuscript of a renowned Jewish physician in Egypt from the twelfth century." The physician is not otherwise specified, but readers could hardly be blamed for supposing him to be Maimonides. Seven years later, the prayer was printed in a Hebrew periodical, *Ha-Me'assef,* accompanied by a statement that its author was the well-known German doctor Marcus Herz, who had requested that the prayer be translated from its original German. According to Dr. Fred Rosner, who is America's foremost authority on the medical writings of Moses Maimonides, the controversy about authorship seems to have begun in 1900, when a state medical journal, *Transactions of the Medical Society of West Virginia*, published excerpts from the prayer along with an article by a Dr. William Golden stating that Maimonides had written it. But Dr. Golden seems to have obtained his text of the prayer from a book called *Justice to the Jews,* written by the pastor of New York's Bloomingdale Church, Reverend Madison C. Peters, in which no authorship is attributed. Golden apparently had second thoughts about his claim: In 1914, he inquired of the editor of the *American Israelite* whether anyone had knowledge of the prayer's source. His reply came from Dr. Gotthard Deutsch, whose first sentences provided a definitive answer to the question: "This so-called prayer of Maimonides is an old hoax. It was actually written by Marcus Herz, a prominent physician of Berlin (1747–1803) who attended Moses Mendelssohn in his last illness." Deutsch attributed the confusion to the fact that Julius Pagel, the most distinguished historian of medicine at the time, had taken the erroneous claim from a colleague's 1875 book without questioning it, and then published the prayer in a Maimonides memorial volume in 1908. Once the Pagel imprimatur was on it, wrote Deutsch, "its authenticity could no more be doubted than the authenticity of the gospel of St. John. . . . No amount of argument will rob Maimonides of the credit for having written this typically lemonade-sweet prayer, characteristic of the era of the Aufklaerung [Enlightenment]." By this time, the prayer had been translated into many European languages, usually attributed to Maimonides. Its first English version had appeared as early as 1841. Deutsch did not have to add that there is no mention or other evidence of the prayer's existence prior to 1783.

Deutsch's letter did not stop the ever-growing tide of attribution to the Rambam. While it has been correctly stated to the point of tedium that the sentiments expressed in the prayer are characteristic of so many statements distributed widely among the medical and nonmedical works of Maimonides, it also evident that certain of the concepts, such as the notion of progress, are inconsistent with medieval thought, not coming to prominence until the Enlightenment. While there is no certainty that Herz was indeed the author, he very probably was. A bit of circumstantial evidence is Herz's letter, writing of a prayer that he openly attributed to himself under the title *Tefillat ha-Rofe* (The Physician's Prayer), containing sentiments similar to those of the 1783 publication. Having tracked down the prayer's entire history and documented every phase of the argument, Rosner must be given the last word.

> The evidence overwhelmingly favors the concept that the physician's prayer attributed to Maimonides is a spurious work, not written by Maimonides but composed by an eighteenth-century writer, probably Marcus Herz. Absolute proof that this is so is, however, lacking and may never be discovered.

This came as hard news to me when I chanced upon Rosner's thoroughgoing analysis while thumbing through an old copy of the *Bulletin of the History of Medicine* some twenty years after its original publication in 1967. For more than a decade, I had kept, always at my elbow on the desk where I work at home, a plaque on which the prayer was inscribed. I hardly considered its words "lemonade-sweet." They inspired me when spirits flagged; they gave me a sense of continuity with physicians everywhere and always. The prayer's final paragraph elevated my sense of worthiness to the task I had chosen. Had Maimonides ever read it, I feel certain it would have done the same for him. I would have preferred that these were indeed his words, but it hardly matters. This prayer is a credo for the life that was his, and has been mine. Any thoughtful physician might say the same.

# Epilogue

U ntil prohibited by the Egyptian government after the founding of the State of Israel in 1948, it was the custom of some of the poorer Jewish families of Cairo to come with their desperately sick to the old synagogue of Maimonides—built two centuries before he first entered it—in the area once called Fustat. The patient, usually one for whom all available therapy had failed, was left to sleep overnight in the underground room, in the hope that he or she would dream of the Rambam and be cured.

The practice of sleeping in a sanctified retreat is at least as old as the pre-Hippocratic period of Greek civilization, when patients of all sorts came to the temples of the god Aesculapius, in the expectation that he would appear to them in a dream and provide the advice that, properly interpreted, would lead to the relief of their infirmities. In the strange mix of faith and healing that characterized the medicine of medieval Christianity, statues of Aesculapius were venerated in some of the early churches as though they were actually statues of Jesus. Not only that, but more than a few early engravings depicting Jesus were modeled on the face of that pagan deity. The faithful flocked to the churches where such images were to be found, seeking to be brought back to health while asleep in the sanctum of prayer. Muslims, too, have their healing saints, whose power is sought through spending the night in certain mosques.

There is a bittersweet irony in the fact that Maimonides, who railed against superstitions of all sorts, should be the object of this one. His is the greatest legend of postbiblical Judaism, and to certain of those whose faith is expressed beyond the bounds of normative theology, his ghostly inter-cession can accomplish anything. For them, it makes no dif-ference that the real Rambam would have condemned the rituals carried out in his name, even as he repeatedly con-demned astrology, amulets, and all such practices that have no basis in reason or the Law. Those who seek his help in these ways are not only fearful and credulous, they are also ignorant of the man and his works. Beyond the legend, he has become a myth.

Of all the aspects of the Rambam's life that have taken on a life of their own, his stature as a man of medicine is the one that most needs to be reconsidered. He was unquestionably a leading clinical physician and medical writer of his time, but his time was one when progress had virtually stopped. He did not transcend, as our greatest innovators have done, the strictures of his era. In fact, he was so much of that era that he epitomized it. And *epitome* would seem to be the perfect word to convey the significance of his contribution to the medicine of the twelfth century—*epitome* in both of its dictionary meanings, as Webster has stated them: "1. a person or thing that is typical of or possesses to a high degree the features of a whole class. 2. a condensed account, esp. of a literary work."

While no less an authority than Sir William Osler, the leading medical luminary of the early twentieth century, famously called Maimonides "the prince of Jewish physicians," the truth would appear to be closer to the far more sober assessment by the eminent Swiss historian of medicine Erwin Ackerknecht, who referred to him as "just another orthodox Galenist." By this he meant that, with the possible exception of Rhazes, doctors of the Arabic period did not do much more than compile and systematize the teachings of Greek medicine, adding only the drugs made available in the lands where they lived and their own personal experience of patient care.

Ackerknecht's judgment, though for the most part accurate, is a bit harsh. It ignores the Rambam's emphasis on ethics and on psychological aspects of illness, which, while hardly original, took on added significance because of his stature as a religious leader and a man from whom the entire world Jewish community sought counsel. It also ignores his literary contribution. Although an epitomizer like all of the renowned Arabic and Jewish physicians of the medieval period, he was an epitomizer with a difference: His talent for distillation of complex and long-winded texts, his ability to clarify abstruse concepts, his purity of prose style that was highly literary while also conversational in voice—these distinctive qualities enabled him to produce concise and highly accessible volumes that must have been extraordinarily useful to the many doctors accustomed to struggling through the textual verbosity of most of his contemporaries. While hardly a step forward in medical science, this alone would have made his name gratefully well recognized in the succeeding centuries.

But we remember and revere Maimonides the physician for quite another reason, far more significant than any contributions he might or might not have made to the science of his time. Paradoxically, it is the myth of him that has been his most powerful medical heritage over the ages, the myth of which he would likely have disapproved, as he did of superstition and magic—disapproved, that is, until he looked at it with the pragmatic eye he so often applied to the problems he faced as the leader of the Jewish community. So focused was he on the reality of his people's continuity that he certainly would have recognized and acknowledged the importance of his enduring stature as the ultimate expression of the Jewish relationship to the art of healing. His name and the imagined majesty of his position in the history of medicine have been an unchanging source of inspiration to Jewish physicians in the eight centuries since his death. His memory is the centrum around which many of them manifest the heritage of doctoring that is the focus of their communal sense of responsibility to repair the world. When I attended a meeting of a newly formed Maimonides

Medical Society in a small North Carolina city some years ago, for example, I was intensely aware of the sense of continuum that united these determined men and women with Jewish doctors everywhere, and with every generation that had preceded them; I was intensely aware of a palpable pride in their willingness to fulfill the ancient obligation derived from the teachings of Torah and Talmud, although they may not have been aware of it—an obligation in their minds originating in the teachings of the Rambam. Whatever mundane considerations and necessities might have blighted their actual functioning in the hurly-burly, commercialized world in which medicine is nowadays practiced, they were sons and daughters of Maimonides on that evening. For at least the moment in which they came together, the legend of the Rambam was living on in their dedication to the healing of the sick; his mythology was nurturing the tradition.

And that may ultimately be the real reason that Maimonides has been an ageless icon to Jews everywhere. It is not the *Commentary on the Mishnah* or the *Mishneh Torah*, although these are still studied by certain Jewish thinkers; it is certainly not *The Guide for the Perplexed*, so much of which is virtually incomprehensible to all but knowledgeable scholars. Rather, it is the iconic memory of a man whose life was devoted to the continuity of the Jewish people.

And in that motivation, I believe, lies the explanation for his life's work—his life's work and the details of his personal responses to difficult times. From the letter to the Jews of Fez, written when he was twenty-four years old, to his labors until the hour of his death as his community's acknowledged leader, he devoted the totality of his prodigious talents to the preservation of the community of Jews everywhere. Viewed from this perspective, his three major writings, as well as the responsa and his public and private actions, can be regarded as a seamless whole. The *Commentary on the Mishnah* brought Judah ha-Nasi's seminal work within the intellectual reach of all Jews, so that they might be reminded—at a time when the future of Jewish life was being threatened on all sides; when there had been an erosion of scholarship and observance; when conversion to Islam or Christianity was common; when knowledge of Hebrew was lessening; when Judaism itself was faltering— of who they were, and of the solidarity inherent in their ancient tradition and code of Law. In the letter to the Jews of Fez, he had already provided rationalizations to help them endure the physical and theological dangers that beset them, and now he was giving them a communal sense of the tradition of order and a set of instructions to unify the straggling elements that threatened to disperse them. As young as he was, he spoke with the certainty necessary to one who would undertake the responsibility of leadership. A self-confidence born of his family's long history of intellectual prominence as well as his own eclectic and intensive education were the instruments by which he so readily assumed the stature of command intrinsic to his success as both the leader of the Jews and their spokesman to the Muslim leaders.

The absolute height of the Rambam's mission to enhance

his people's unity was achieved in the writing of the *Mishneh Torah*, the constitution through which all Jews who could but read Hebrew were provided with a code by which to live the distinctive life demanded by their membership in the community. They could be united by the very fact of the demands made on them, which enhanced their cohesion not only to a common set of principles but to one another and to the whole. Its synoptic message was expressed in its coming to be called *Yad ha-Hazakah* (The Strong Hand), which was in fact the strong hand of the Rambam, directing his people toward the cohesion that would preserve it.

But as distinctive as Judaism must remain, it must also live in the intellectual world surrounding it. From childhood, young Moses had been enthralled by the philosophy of Aristotle and by the knowledge then available of science, realizing as well that such principles were becoming increasingly significant in the thought of leading non-Jewish scholars and the interpretation of their scriptures. Already having introduced the elements of philosophy and science into his earlier writings so that they would be known to his general readers, he recognized that the most educated of them—those who were well versed in both faith and reason—must perceive inconsistencies with which Maimonides had himself grappled and resolved, or at least resolved insofar as such a thing was possible. If enlightened intellects like these were not to lose their commitment to Judaism, and, moreover, if Judaism was to take its place among the religious systems not scorned as archaic by the emerging thinkers of Islam and Christianity, its theology must incorporate the wisdom of the Greeks—an attempt must be made to demonstrate its compatibility with the methods and logic of the Aristoteleans. Not only was it in the Rambam's conception of Judaism that it must be progressive, but that in its very progress lay one of the keys to its continuity.

Essays and books have been written and debates have proliferated about the real reason why Maimonides wrote the *Guide*. Should his words be taken at face value—that he undertook the project to help Joseph ibn Aknin in his quest for reconciliation between faith and reason? But since so much of the book is specifically *not* meant to be taken at face value, since so much of it is deliberately obscured from direct view, is there some other agenda? Some have gone so far as to suggest that the Rambam was a variety of crypto-agnostic who hid his skepticism from public view but here was revealing it to those who could decode his message. He had solved the conflict between faith and reason by abjuring faith and joining himself completely to reason, say those who take this view, and the *Guide* was at once his confession and his attempt to convince the few qualified others to do the same.

I would argue that such considerations are spurious. The notion of complete incongruity between reason and science on the one hand and faith on the other is a concept that did not fully come into being until the Enlightenment of the eighteenth century. To argue that Maimonides had somehow lost his religious belief and was now secretly leading others toward a position based solely on reason is untenable. The philosophical problem of the era in which he lived was to find a conciliation between faith and reason, engaging thinkers as disparate in background as Abelard in Paris and Averroës in Cordoba. If there was a single figure of the age who rejected religion in the cause of philosophy and science—as many would do five and six centuries later—no one knows his name. What the Rambam did throughout all of his writings—long before he composed the *Guide*—was to attempt an incorporation of philosophy and science into religious thought, not only because he was convinced that it belonged but also because he was bringing a progressive worldview to his theology. Whatever else this latter motive might accomplish, it could serve the purpose of bringing Jewish ways of religious perception closer to what we would today call mainstream thought. To him, such a consideration not only made theological sense but was a means of his people's survival.

There remains the question of why the *Guide* was written in such a way that assured its obscurity to all but a few, if its purpose was not to hide its author's putative loss of faith from all but those who might sympathize with such a position. Before engaging this question, it needs to be pointed out that Maimonides lived in an age when writing in encoded messages was not uncommon, because it was sometimes dangerous to do otherwise in such hostile surroundings. Unfortunately, acquiring the intellectual wherewithal to decode the *Guide* requires having the detailed knowledge possessed by a highly educated twelfth-century Jewish mind of a certain sort, which means that modern-day or future attempts to fully fathom the text must of necessity be doomed to some degree of failure regardless of the sophistication brought to the enterprise or the claims made by those who have in recent centuries written wise disquisitions. One should not have pretensions to overcoming the impossible.

There is no ready answer to the greater question of why it is that only those qualified to understand the abstruse message were to be addressed. But there are certain circumstantial hints. There had long been much criticism, some of it quite bitter, of Maimonides' inclusion of principles of philosophy and science in the *Commentary on the Mishnah* and the *Mishneh Torah*. In writing the *Guide*, perhaps he had decided to deal at last with the fact that only a very few people of his era had enough intellectual sophistication to comprehend the validity of his insights. By this time, he may no longer have cared to be understood by those others who would once again only use his words as arguments against him and against the acceptance of his message. In a sense, he was deliberately preaching to a very select congregation, promulgating notions that were still new and hard to accept. Better to write in ways that only the select few could interpret than to be exposed to the abuse of the many. A more straightforward style would only have been counterproductive. If philosophy and science were to be incorporated into Jewish theology, only the intellectual elite could accomplish it.

Some observers of his life have spoken of the two Moses ben Maimons: the one who wrote the first two of the three great books in a clear style meant for general readers, and the other one who wrote the *Guide* meant only for the elect. There are even those among the deeply Orthodox who would have no truck with the *Guide*. A few go so far as to call its author by his Greek name of Maimonides, reserving the appellation "the Rambam" for the revered Jewish sage whose responsa and two books they consult to solve halakhic disputes.

They are deluding themselves. For the reasons just given, it would seem highly unlikely that the earlier Moses had lost his direction and become the later one. It is far more probable that he had simply changed the focus of his goal and his perception of the best way to carry out his self-ordained mission to preserve his people and bring their belief into harmony with philosophy and science.

Perhaps Maimonides had lost not religious faith but faith in ordinary men to do what must be done. After all, he had again and again declared in various ways that ordinary men are not equipped to grasp ultimate theological truth. Perhaps his writing the *Guide* the way he did was an indication that he was turning his attention exclusively to those who he hoped would take on the leadership. In succeeding generations or centuries, it would be their obligation to gradually find ways by which the truth might be revealed to the greater society. He had lost not only faith in those of his contemporaries who walked in what he called "the path of fools," but patience, too, and he did not wish to undergo yet more scrutiny and criticism by men he judged to be unqualified, who might stand in the way of the necessary reform in thought. Recall the words of the *Guide*'s introduction, quoted above: "I am a man who— . . . if he knows no other way to teach a proven truth except by appealing to one chosen man, even if failing to appeal to ten thousand fools— prefers imparting the truth to this one man."

Viewed in this way—the way of a towering intellect determined to keep the Jewish people together during dreadfully dangerous times and to restore its religiosity by appealing to both ancient and progressive impulses (in other words, appealing to the masses and then later to the elect who might ultimately disseminate that religious philosophy and thereby ensure survival)—all other considerations dissolve into disorganized polemic. Rabbi Moses labored mightily for his cause, accomplishing feats of sheer endurance that would tax the energies of ordinary men, until he finally exhausted his life in the effort.

Since the Rambam's death on that December day eight hundred years ago, a long series of scholars has attempted to do with his heritage what I, in my own unscholarly way, have been attempting in this book. His life, his work, his motivations, and his legacy have been constantly resifted and rethought. In every era, attempts have been made to find a

Maimonides for that time and even that place—and no doubt for that seeker. Through the mists of eight centuries of history and the multiple prisms of every previous commentator, no one can be sure if, in the words of Rabbi Hertzberg, we are finding Maimonides "as he would have wanted us to learn from him" or the Maimonides that "we want to hear." I suspect it to be far more the latter than the former.

The rabbis elucidating the meaning of Torah did much the same when they compiled the Mishnah and Gemara. And like the ancient Jewish dictum that one is not permitted to turn away from a responsibility, the dictum to find evolving meaning in a text is as great as the dictum to perceive that it contains certain immutable truths that do not change. Like the Torah and the Talmud that we see in the light of our needs and our times, the life of Maimonides will always reveal more, the more it is studied. The great sages set the pattern when they said, *"Dor dor v'dorshav"*—"Each generation should bring forth its own interpreters." Every reader of this book can follow in that path.

In doing so, each of us seeks a truth that is universal but is in fact very probably ours alone. In seeking the truth of Maimonides, we try to separate the verifiable facts from the speculations and finally from the myths. But we should not let go of the myths entirely, not only because they arise from a legend whose ultimate basis is the truth of his life, but also because myths satisfy the imagination within us that craves flights of fancy no matter their magical unlikelihood. And here I offer one that has no less basis in reality than the tale of the ten-year-old preacher or of the coffin that could not be lifted by an entire band of Bedouins. Think, if you will, of that day on which the scroll of the Rambam's life was completed, and imagine him being gathered to his seven generations of rabbinic forebears—and their unnamed wives and daughters—in *Olam ha-Ba*. On his arrival in that celestial place that may not be a physical place, they would then join the biblical Moses himself in greeting his namesake's appearance that may not be a physical appearance, with joyous shouts of *Hazak! Hazak! V'nit'hazeik!* "Be strong! Be strong! And may we be strengthened!"

# APPENDIX

## The Medical Works of Maimonides

Three of the ten medical treatises of Maimonides have been discussed in the chapter titled "Maimonides, Physician." The other seven books deal with clinical matters. In describing them, I have followed the classification used by Dr. Max Meyerhof, who studied each of the original texts and is given credit by other scholars for verifying the origin and authenticity of several of them.

A short treatise on hemorrhoids (seventy-three pages in a twentieth-century English translation) was written at the request of an unnamed young man from a noble Cairo family. The Maimonidean approach to a disease that in those days could have extremely serious consequences—such as anemia, chronic protein deficiency, and even death—was conservative, reserving surgery (consisting of ligature or the application of the red-hot iron) or bleeding for extreme cases. Stressing the importance of constipation as a cause, Maimonides recommended a diet high in roughage, a therapy with which no present-day proctologist would find fault. None of this is original with the author, the entire work being based on a chapter in Avicenna's *Canon* written early in the eleventh century, a book generally regarded as the greatest medical text of the Middle Ages.

Also based on the *Canon*, and on every other medical book since the days of Hippocrates and even before, was Maimonides' notion about the cause of the hemorrhoidal disease. He believed it to be most commonly due to an excess of black bile, which thickens and sinks down into the lowermost reaches of the pelvis, by pressure stretching the blood vessels around the rectum and anus, thereby causing them to protrude. As though writing today, he recommends that various salves and unguents, including zinc oxide ointment, be applied. But being a physician of the twelfth century, he also suggests fumigation of the anal orifice, which he says is particularly useful in combating the flatulence that so often accompanies the ailment.

As fumigations of various sorts were frequent remedies for a variety of bowel, urinary, and uterine disabilities in the Middle Ages and for centuries afterward, a brief aside may be justified here to illustrate not only a typical intervention of the time, but also the sort of botanicals and animal agents involved in it, and the ways in which they were employed. Maimonides begins his description by listing a choice of ten pharmacologic agents (they range from snakeskin to gum of juniper), one or several of which are to be kneaded into an appropriate volume of honey. A fire is then started within the confines of a hole dug in the ground, into which the compounded drug is then thrown. At this point, the patient seats himself on an upended earthenware pot whose bottom is perforated to allow the resultant fumes to pass through it and upward into his anus. The subject is to huddle his loose garments closely around the pot and the excavation beneath it, to be sure that none of the healing vapors escapes anywhere but through the hole and up into his nether orifice. By this means would the hemorrhoids be dried and obliterated, claims the text.

Another of the small treatises of Maimonides was his little book on poisons, written at the request of el Fadil in 1198. Snake and insect bites were a constant danger throughout the Muslim lands, and many Arabic authors had written about their treatment, as well as those of mad dogs. Here Maimonides does the same. It is clear from his description of the symptoms of such poisonings that he had had plenty of experience with them. He properly recommends that some wounds not be immediately dressed, in order to allow free escape of venom from the site of injury. A tourniquet above an extremity bite is suggested to prevent dissemination via the bloodstream, and the area is to be incised for optimal drainage. If suction by dry cups seems insufficient, the physician may suck the venom away with his lips after rinsing the mouth—which must be free of sores and infected teeth—with a mixture of wine and oil. In any event, one must anoint the inside of the mouth with olive oil before attempting the procedure. When indicated, the wound may be cauterized with a hot iron. Maimonides' discussion of the antidotes then in use reveals to a modern eye none that appears to have any specific efficacy. Included in the definition of poisons are those drug remedies for various illnesses that should be avoided or used with extreme care because they may be dangerous to life. The usefulness of this small volume is indicated by the fact that its Latin translation was quoted frequently in the writings of the two most prominent surgeons of the thirteenth and fourteenth centuries, respectively, Henri de Mondeville and Guy de Chauliac of France.

Yet another book written for a patient of high rank (referred to as His Highness, the Prince, and thought to have been al Afdal) is the *Discourse on Asthma*, in which Maimonides treats his unnamed patient's specific symptoms of chest pain and headache so severe that he is unable to wear a turban. Of course, we cannot be sure that the disease being written about is really asthma as we know it today, although its description is similar. Once again, dietary changes are recommended, among which a modern reader may not be surprised to find chicken soup, a remedy that appears in other of the author's books as well. But the part of the *Discourse* most interesting today is the discussion of climatic effects on the disease, emphasizing the benefits of dry air. In Egypt, he points out, the climate is so dry that dietary measures are not necessary. In addition, he asserts that the pure air of the countryside is much more healthful than that of the polluted city. Although these are hardly great insights, one of the values of the book is its author's reiteration of his theme of the avoidance of strong remedies, whether drugs, purging, or surgery. This book was translated into Hebrew and Latin, but there were no editions in European languages until relatively recent times.

Many physicians living in the Arabic lands—as many as several hundred between the ninth and thirteenth centuries—wrote treatises on sexual matters, and Maimonides is no exception. Such works appear to have been very popular among men of the nobility and prominent families, those who might ask a well-known doctor to write one for a specific purpose, such as the enhancement of his performance in the harem. Men at this social level usually had at least several wives, and tending to the needs of these ever-competitive women was not only irresistible but frequently exhausting. Although the person who approached Maimonides with such a request is not named, he has been thought to be a nephew of Saladin, Sultan Al Muzaffar Umar ibn Nur ad Din, who ruled in Hamah, Syria, from 1179 to 1192. The book, *On Sexual Intercourse*, has already been briefly discussed in a previous chapter, but its details are well worth reviewing as a window on the specificity of Maimonidean medical counsel.

The volume's nineteen short chapters cover a variety of facets of sexual activity, ranging from those remedies that abet desire and performance to those that keep it in check lest it enervate body and soul. Because some of this enervation seems to have already overtaken the subject of the book, he is seeking advice on ways to keep up with his urges and his wives. The patron, writes Maimonides in the first chapter of his treatise, "has instructed me to prepare for him a guide to aid him in the increase of sexual intercourse, since he mentioned that he has need thereof, and his nature tends somewhat towards heat. He reports, may the Lord preserve his power, that he desires to give up nothing of his habits in connection with sexual intercourse, although the servant [Maimonides] has called attention to the meagerness of the lord's body, so that he is near emaciation. He desires this addition on account of the increase of a large number of concubines."

Maimonides' advice is wide-ranging, and he quotes, as is usual in his medical writings, Galen and many Arabic authors. This is all to the good, because it is difficult to believe that personal experience played any major role in the recommendations recorded in this particular volume of the great sage's medical works. And it is also difficult to believe that such counsel comes from a man who elsewhere (*On the Regulation of Health*) wrote, "Sexual intercourse harms most people. . . .Whoever wishes to remain healthy should shake the idea of sexual intercourse from his mind as much as he can." And yet, every knowledgeable commentator on the medical writings of Maimonides insists that he never recommended a treatment unless he had tried it for safety on himself, which, if true, must in this case have been a bit of an ordeal for a man so committed to Torah and scholarship. Or perhaps not.

Nevertheless, Maimonides' own convictions did not deter him from coming up with the requested remedy. To provide it, he quotes from Avenzoar and a few others in addressing an age-old concern of concupiscent men. Any doubts that Maimonides was a physician of his time should be dispelled by reading the following paragraph:

> And he [presumably Avenzoar] also says: Since there are many people who would want to have an erection lasting for a considerable period of time, even after, by ejaculation, the flow of sperm has been decreased, it is proper that I should mention this. It is a great secret, which no one has as yet mentioned previously. Carrot oil and radish oil, of each one liter, mustard oil one quarter liter. Mix it all and place therein live yellow ants one half liter. Put the oil in the sun for four to seven days and then avail yourself of it as oil for the glans of the penis two or three hours before sexual intercourse. Behold, it remains in erection even after the emission of the sperm. Nothing comparable has been done in this area.

One of the most remarkable of the books of Maimonides is a recently discovered volume of uncertain date called *Glossary of Drug Names*, in which the author lists in alphabetical order some two thousand agents whose names appear in the contemporary medical literature, the great majority being botanicals, although there are some of animal or mineral derivation. In most cases he provides the Arabic name of the drug followed by synonyms in the same language and then equivalents—where they exist—in Greek, Syriac, Persian,

Berber, and Spanish. No Hebrew names of the agents appear, which is thought by scholars to mean that the book was intended primarily for the use of non-Jewish pupils and colleagues. Because Maimonides frequently repeats the words "in our land, al-Maghrib" (the west, a term used for North Africa and Spain), he very likely wrote this treatise during his time in Morocco or shortly thereafter. Clearly, this repeated reference might be interpreted as an indication that he was even at that early time beginning to think about the practice of medicine. As useful as this book should have been to physicians in various countries, it seems never to have been translated into other languages until modern times. In fact, not even a Hebrew edition has been found.

Reflecting on this book, one cannot but be struck by the enormous amount of meticulous work that must have been involved in producing it, not to mention the sheer dogged effort required. Vast numbers of text pages had to have been scrutinized, repetitions weeded out (pun intended), and synonyms tracked down from a multiplicity of sources. Again and again in the writings of this gifted scholar, the reader is overwhelmed by his extraordinary ability to gather vast numbers of not-necessarily-connected facts while at the same time organizing them into a whole that is not only coherent, but synthesizes the accumulation of knowledge into all-encompassing theses and common principles. He does it in his medical writings, he does it in his philosophical and scientific writings, and he does it in his religious writings.

The treatise thought to be the last written by Maimonides is his very brief *Discourse on the Explanation of Fits*, composed at the behest of al Afdal in 1200, when its author was already in ill health and unable to attend personally on the ruler. The fits referred to are fits of melancholy, for which al Afdal had been seen by other of his physicians without a resolution of the problem.

The sultan had the results of these consultations brought to Maimonides in Fustat, who reviewed them and sent back twenty-two paragraphs of recommendations, the first eighteen of which commented on the advice previously rendered by his colleagues. He confirmed much of it, but when he disagreed he did so in the gentle, noncritical manner that was his way. The nineteenth and twentieth paragraphs consist of general statements about the best regimen in such cases. The twenty-first prescribes an hour-by-hour routine to be followed each day, including mild medications and riding in the morning, an appropriate, easily digestible repast, and then an afternoon nap accompanied by soft singing and the playing of a stringed instrument. Reading and pleasant conversation are to follow, after which a light supper and a little wine are taken, and then a few hours of music until drowsiness puts the patient into a comfortable sleep. The aim is clearly to regulate the day so carefully that the patient is always occupied, distracted from the obsessive thoughts that so often overtake the depressed when they have the opportunity to ruminate.

The twenty-second paragraph, which is really a concluding vote of confidence in the patient that he will know how best to implement these recommendations, is of interest for a sentence that some scholars have thought to reveal, in Meyerhof's words, "a conflict between Maimonides the physician and Maimonides the theologian." This is the healer's apology for recommending wine and music to al Afdal, which the physician realizes "are abominated by the religious law." The passage goes on to state, "Religion prescribes all that is useful and forbids all that is harmful in the next world; while the doctor indicates what is useful and warns against what is harmful in this world." Those who see deeper meaning in these words consider them a rationalization used by Maimonides in his lifelong attempt to accommodate matters of faith with matters of science or philosophy. More likely, it was simply his way of avoiding any implied offense to his royal patron and also of making it easier for al Afdal to follow his recommendations.

Another passage of interest in the *Discourse* is the following: "I have had occasion to treat some patients whose disease followed the way of the King's suffering from melancholy, which is to say that it turns into mania, that is raving madness." While it is always dangerous to diagnose from minimal evidence provided in text from long ago, one cannot help but wonder whether al Afdal suffered from the problem nowadays called bipolar disorder.

In 1198, a messenger had come to Maimonides from the thirty-year-old al Afdal just after he had ascended to the throne, asking him, in the words of the physician's response, "to write down the regimen he should follow in the treatment of the diseases that befell my lord." The "diseases" were said by the messenger to consist of "chronic difficult bowel movements that take place only after strenuous effort, . . . occasional attacks of horror, melancholy and the fear of death. This is accompanied by vomiting and poor digestion most of the time." To a modern-day physician, such symptoms suggest that the sultan was suffering from chronic depression with occasional panic attacks, which seem to have been an occupational disease of the Arab rulers of that day.

Al Afdal was known as a profligate, pleasure-pursuing man whose intrigues got him into frequent conflicts, including some with his own relatives. He suffered for his habits, not only with the disabling symptoms he reported to Maimonides, but also with a brief reign, lasting from his ascension, shortly before seeking this medical advice, until 1200. Very likely, he did not follow the suggestions made to him, being so wedded to habits that were physically, emotionally, and politically hazardous.

The physician's response took the form of a short— ninety small pages in a modern English translation— treatise called by either of two names, *On the Regulation of Health* or *The Preservation of Youth* (*Regimen Sanitatis* in Latin). Though directed to the care of a single individual, this useful little book became widely read and quoted. Numerous Arabic manuscripts of it have been found, attesting to its wide popularity and what we nowadays call the "name

recognition" of its author. There were also two Latin translations, the second one—in 1477—being the first medical
book ever published in Florence. Later editions of these
Latin texts appeared as late as the one published in Lyons in
1535. In that era when knowledge was not advancing and the
same books were read unchanged for generations and longer,
doctors continued to refer to *Regimen Sanitatis* throughout
the Middle Ages and beyond. Already well known in the
world of Arabic medicine, the reputation of Maimonides
was further enhanced by its appearance.

The first two of the book's four chapters provide general
advice for maintaining health and treating sickness, by and
large employing the standard methods used since the times
of Hippocrates and Galen. The third chapter addresses the
sultan's complaints, beginning with a paragraph worth
reproducing here in its entirety because it echoes a thesis
that is older than the pyramids (the Egyptians had an entire
mythology of the rectum, based on the dangers of the fecal
effluvium they called *wehuduw*) and continues to be an article
of faith in the minds of millions of people who believe that
retained stool poisons the system.

It has been the consensus of medical opinion that
the foundation of health is that the excrements should
be soft, and if they are hard one should make them
soft. Their retention produces very bad fumes that
enter the heart and the brain and cause dehydration
and confusion of the vital spirits. They produce bad

thoughts, apprehensions and exhaustion, and prevent
the elimination of superfluities from digested materials. A special effort is needed to soften the stool.

Having made that statement, Maimonides then goes on to
discuss such standard topics as treatments for constipation;
the role of the liver in health; ways of strengthening the
heart; and drugs that function as digestives, aphrodisiacs,
and sedatives. These are all matters that might be found in
any book of medical advice of the time. But in the third
chapter of the text, a change in tone takes place, from the
traditional Galenic voice to the voice that is distinctly that
of Maimonides. Whereas the usual Arabic authority would
at this point likely proceed to a mind-numbing catalogue
and description of botanical agents to treat the sultan's psychological symptoms, this healer takes a different tack, typical of his distinctive approach.

The very first sentence of this section of the treatise
sets the mood for the rest: "My lord, let God prolong his
days, should know that emotional experiences cause marked
changes in the body which are clear and visible to all and
bear witness in clear testimony." The text continues, stressing the importance of the emotional equilibrium that pre-
vents illness. It deals directly with the seeming paradox of al
Afdal himself, a powerful ruler who seemingly has all that
any man might desire but is nevertheless burdened by black
thoughts and physical symptoms. What would appear to be
the goods and evils of the world, Maimonides says, are actu-

ally imaginary goods and evils, especially when emotions are labile and not in a state of equanimity and balance.

How often does there fall to someone's share a great fortune or prominence and power, and it is this that causes the decay of his body and the deterioration of his soul and character, shortens his life and alienates him from his Creator, the Most High. What an eternal misfortune is this for him! On the other hand, how often does someone lose his fortune or a king his power, and it is this that strengthens his body, perfects his soul with moral qualities, prolongs his life, brings him nearer to the Lord, and incites him to devotion to His service.

The final chapter of the book returns to the standard Greek recommendations about wholesome food, clean air and water, and the importance of sunshine, with the added admonition that one not rush into treatment for every minor ailment because "Nature takes care of all these things and one need not have recourse to medication." (Eight centuries later, the eminent researcher and medical writer Lewis Thomas would write, "The great secret, known to internists and learned early in marriage by internists' wives, but still hidden from the general public, is that most things get better by themselves. Most things, in fact, are better by morning.")

Hidden away in this chapter are a few sentences about the difficulty of practicing the art of medicine, and, in fact, of any scientific pursuit. Maimonides here makes a statement that will resonate with every experienced physician or researcher who reads it. It would seem appropriate to conclude this appendix on his medical writings with a statement that is timeless:

> The more perfect a person becomes in one of the sciences, the more cautious he grows, developing doubts, questions and problems that are only partially solved. And the more deficient one is in science, the easier it will be for him to understand every difficulty, making the improbable probable and increasing the false claims which he represents as certain knowledge, and is eager to explain things that he does not understand himself.

# CHRONOLOGY

360 B.C.E.  Death of Hippocrates, father of medicine.

322 B.C.E.  Death of Aristotle, Greek philosopher whose rational approach was great influence on both philosophy and science.

c. 100 C.E.  Rufus of Samaria, earliest known Jewish physician, writes commentary on Hippocrates; is quoted by Galen.

c. 200 C.E.  Galen of Pergamon codifies medicine based on the Hippocratic School, with great advances in experimentation and physiology.

c. 200 C.E.  Rabbi Judah ha-Nasi codifies the Mishnah as a compendium of Jewish law.

1020  Avicenna, the most prominent physician of the Muslim world, serves as court physician to various Arab rulers; his greatest work, *The Canon of Medicine*, is used in Europe through the seventeenth century.

1070  Rashi, Rabbi Samuel ben Isaac, composes commentaries on most of the Bible and the

Talmud. Endures as one of the greatest and most influential Jewish scholars.

1095 The First Crusade begins; Jews are murdered in Speyer, Worms, Mainz, and Cologne.

1099 Godfrey of Bouillon conquers Jerusalem, where Jews and Karaites are massacred.

1135 The Rashbam, Rabbi Samuel ben Meir, grandson of Rashi, writes commentary on Torah using literal/textual approach.

Council of Rheims forbids monks and clergy from practicing medicine as contrary to Christian theology.

1138 Moses son of Maimon, later known as Maimonides, is born on 14th of the Hebrew month of Nisan, Passover eve (corresponding to March 30 on the Gregorian calendar) in Cordoba; his mother dies in childbirth.

c. 1138–1147 Rabbi Maimon, father of Maimonides, remarries; three more children are born: David, Miriam, and another daughter whose name is unknown.

1139 Rabbi Judah ha-Levi publishes the *Kuzari*, a polemic in defense of Judaism written in the

form of a dialogue between a rabbi and the king
of the Khazars; dies the following year in Israel.

1140   The Tosafists, Rashi's grandsons, write
       commentary seeking to resolve apparent
       contradictions among Rashi, the Talmud, the
       Bible, and other commentators.

       Rabbi Abraham ibn Ezra, author of rationalist
       and linguistic commentaries, leaves Spain; first
       to hint at non-Mosaic origin of some biblical
       verses.

1144   First blood libel, in Norwich, England; Jews are
       accused of murdering a Christian child and
       using his blood for ritual purposes.

1146   Second Crusade launched, to aid besieged
       Christian Kingdom of Jerusalem.

1148   Following Almohads' invasion of Cordoba,
       Maimon family flees to Almeria, where Moses is
       thought to have befriended Muslim
       philosopher ibn Rushd, known as Averroës. An
       interpreter of Aristotle and medical adviser to
       chief judge of Cordoba, Averroës, like
       Maimonides, later attempts to reconcile faith
       with Aristotelean philosophy.

       King Louis VII and leaders of Second Crusade
       assemble in Jerusalem. Further massacres of
       Jews.

c. 1148–1158  As Maimon family wanders Spain, Maimonides composes works including *Millot Higayon*, an introduction to logic based on Aristotle, and *Ma'amar ha-Ibbur*, about the Hebrew calendar; researches the work of the Geonim (arbiters of Jewish law in the sixth through tenth centuries) and collects teachings of his father and of his teacher, Joseph ibn Migas.

1151  Maimon family flees Almeria following advance of Almohads.

1158  Maimonides begins writing the *Kitab al-Siraj*, *Commentary on the Mishnah*.

1160  Maimon family moves to Fez. Rabbi Maimon writes *Letter of Consolation*, reassuring the Jews of Morocco that even if they must outwardly live as Muslims in order to survive, the God of Israel would still hear their prayers.

1160  Rabad, Rabbi Abraham ben David, founds academy in Posquières; preeminent legal authority of Jews of Provence, critic of Maimonides.

1162  Maimonides writes *Letter on Conversion*, in which he marshals the sources of Jewish law to show that outward conversion to Islam is

permissible under the dire circumstances in
which many Jews were then living.

1163 Abd al-Mumin, caliph of Fez, dies; succeeded
by much harsher ruler, Abu Yakub Yusuf.

1165 Maimonides arrested for relapsing to Judaism
after ostensibly converting to Islam; released
on testimony of his friend Abul Arab ibn
Moisha.

Rabbi Judah ibn Shoshan, leader of the Jews of
Fez, is executed on charge of reverting to
Judaism after converting to Islam.

Maimon family escapes Fez; hides in Ceuta en
route to Palestine.

Maimon family arrives in Palestine in May or
June. After a brief stay, they move to Alexandria.

Death of Rabbi Maimon. Maimonides assumes
leadership of the family.

1168 *Commentary on the Mishnah* is completed.
Maimonides and his family move to Fustat.

1169 Saladin becomes vizier of Egypt.

1170 Maimonides completes *Sefer ha-Mitzvot*, an
enumeration of the 613 commandments; begins
to compose *Mishneh Torah*, his great law code.

Jews of Tudela move into citadel for protection; Spanish king grants them right of self-defense.

1171  Blood libel comes to European continent, appearing first in Blois, France.

Saladin deposes Fatimid sultan and returns Egypt to Abbassid house of Baghdad, which will rule until 1250. Saladin's rule is noted for his compassion toward minorities under his sovereignty.

1172  Shiite oppression of Jews in Yemen increases.

Maimonides writes *Letter to Yemen*, reassuring the Jews of Yemen that the Jewish people and their unique relationship with God will endure.

Benjamin of Tudela returns from his travels around the Mediterranean coast, the Arabian peninsula, and North Africa; his account of his journeys is the greatest resource for information on the scattered Jewish community in this period.

1174  Maimonides' brother, David, dies on voyage to India; Maimonides sinks into prolonged depression.

Saladin takes power in Syria; prepares to battle Crusader forces.

Turhan Shah, brother of Saladin, takes control in Yemen, releasing Jews from Shiite oppression.

1175  Maimonides marries daughter of Rabbi Mishael Halevi of Fustat; her name is unrecorded.

Maimonides begins to practice medicine.

c. 1176–1184  Daughter born to Maimonides and his wife; she dies in infancy.

1180  Maimonides completes the *Mishneh Torah*, a compendium of Jewish law.

1182  The Jews of France are expelled by Philip Augustus.

1185  Joseph ibn Aknin comes to Fustat to study with Maimonides.

1186  A son, Abraham, is born to Maimonides and his wife.

1187  Maimonides appointed physician to Egyptian vizier el Fadil.

Joseph ibn Aknin moves to Aleppo.

Abul Arab ibn Moisha denounces Maimonides before tribunal; he is saved by el Fadil's intervention.

Maimonides named *nagid*, chief rabbi, of all lands controlled by Saladin.

1189  Richard I the Lionhearted launches Third
      Crusade.

1190  Saladin conquers Jerusalem from Crusaders,
      permits Jewish resettlement.

      Anti-Jewish riots break out in England.

1190  Maimonides' *The Guide for the Perplexed*, an
      attempt to reconcile faith and reason, is
      completed.

      Joseph ibn Aknin moves to Bagdhad.

1190–1204  Maimonides publishes several medical treatises
      including *The Medical Aphorisms of Moses;* largely
      based on Galen and yet willing to challenge
      him, the *Aphorisms* are used in Muslim lands
      and in Europe for several centuries.

1193  Death of Saladin.

1198  Saladin's son, al Afdal, appoints Maimonides
      chief physician.

1204  Samuel ibn Tibbon completes translation of
      *The Guide for the Perplexed*, called *Moreh Nevukhim*
      in Hebrew.

      December 13, the 20th of the Hebrew month of
      Tevet, Moses Maimonides dies.

1215  Fourth Lateran Council decrees that physicians may not treat patients without presence of Christian clergy.

1290  Jews are expelled from England.

1304  Prominent German rabbis ban study of all philosophy and science except medicine for those less than twenty-five years old.

1335  Rabbi Jacob ben Asher completes the *Arba'ah Turim*, first codification of Jewish law since Mainmonides' *Mishneh Torah*.

1492  Christian conquest of Spain is complete; Jews are expelled.

1543  Andreas Vesalius of Brussels publicly demonstrates significant errors in Galenic anatomy.

1555  Rabbi Joseph Caro completes the *Shulkhan Arukh* (the Set Table), a digest of his commentary on the *Arba'ah Turim*, which quickly becomes the authoritative compilation of Jewish law for the Sephardic community. Shortly thereafter, Rabbi Moses Isserles of Kraków publishes the *Mapah* (Tablecloth), an Ashkenazic addendum to the *Shulkhan Arukh*.

1783 First appearance of Prayer of Maimonides in
German journal *Deutsches Museum*.

1896 Two British travelers in Egypt happen upon
the Cairo *Genizah*, a trove of documents of the
Cairo Jewish community dating back to the
tenth century, including several documents in
Maimonides' own hand. Scholar Solomon
Schechter obtains the papers for Cambridge
University, where his study of them yields a
new understanding of the Egyptian Jewish
community.

1947 Maimonides Hospital in Brooklyn formed from
the mergers of the New Utrecht Infirmary,
Beth Moses Hospital, and Israel Zion Hospital.

1985 First Maimonides Society, an organization of
Jewish doctors, founded in Allentown,
Pennsylvania, under the aegis of the Jewish
Federation; chapters founded under local
Jewish federations nationwide.

# BIBLIOGRAPHICAL NOTES

Several biographies provided me with background information, chronologies of events, and links to the circumstances of the time of Maimonides. Such books supplied a practical context in which to place the settings in which the treatises were written, and to understand how contemporary political and social structures influenced Jewish communities in general and Maimonides in particular. A few of these are volumes I would recommend to readers unacquainted with such material. Primary among them is Abraham Joshua Heschel's *Maimonides* (New York: Farrar, Straus & Giroux, 1982), which roams widely across the spectrum between biography and commentary, sometimes so much so that a beginning reader must be constantly alert to follow the sequence of the story. Nevertheless, it is a very readable book, written in the author's characteristically thoughtful style.

A book of quite another sort is Ilil Arbel's little volume *Maimonides: A Spiritual Biography* (New York: Crossroads, 2001), so straightforward and lucid a description of the events of the Rambam's life that it can be recommended as an introductory text for interested teenagers, being far less spiritual and far more factually absorbing than its title would indicate. Among others of my favorite biographies is one of several written in 1935, during the year until recently thought to be the eight hundredth anniversary of Maimonides' birth, when an outpouring of texts appeared. This is Solomon Zeitlin's *Maimonides: A Biography* (New York: Bloch, 1935).

Other of the books described in the following paragraphs contain sections and essays of biographical information interspersed with content devoted primarily to Maimonides' writings, philosophies, and cultural activities. For those readers wishing to know more about the Andalusian Spain in which Maimonides was born—and the Jewish, Christian, and Muslim luminaries who thrived in that unique time and place—there is no more fascinating and authoritative source than Maria Rosa Menocal's *The Ornament of the World: How Muslims, Jews, and Christians Created a Culture of Tolerance in Medieval Spain* (Boston: Little, Brown, 2002).

Various perspectives of Maimonidean thought and biography are illuminated by reading in volumes of essays composed or edited by authorities on the Rambam's life and works. Although some were written more than half a century ago, they are just as pertinent today as they were at the time of publication (much the same can be said of other of the recommended texts below). Those I've found most helpful have been *Essays in Maimonides*, edited by Salo Baron (New York: Columbia University Press, 1941), and *Moses Maimonides: Anglo-Jewish Papers in Connection with the Eighth Cente-*

*nary of His Birth*, edited by Rabbi I. Epstein (London: Soncino Press, 1935).

I have found it very helpful to read chrestomathies of Maimonides' writings, in which sections of varying length are extracted from his three great treatises, the medical works, letters, and responsa. The majority of the passages quoted in this book come from these sources. My favorite of such collections is Isadore Twersky's *A Maimonides Reader*, published by the Library of Jewish studies in 1972. Professor Twersky's extensive introduction is a particularly useful epitome of Maimonidean thought and the intellectual characteristics that made it so unique. Similar chrestomathies are those brought together by Rabbi Abraham Cohen in *The Teachings of Maimonides* (New York: Ktav, 1968), and by Jacob Minkin, in a volume with the same title (Northvale, N.J.: Jason Aronson, 1987). Both have excellent and wide-ranging introductions, in which are included biographical, theological, and philosophical themes.

To those wrestling with the question of Maimonides' solution to the apparent inconsistency between faith and reason, I can do no better than to suggest consulting two authors who have addressed the problem from differing perspectives. David Hartman's *Maimonides: Torah and Philosophic Quest* (Philadelphia: Jewish Publication Society, 1976) puts forth one viewpoint, and the well-known essay of Leo Strauss, "Notes on Maimonides's Book of Knowledge," in *Studies in Mysticism and Religion*—edited by E. E. Urbach,

R. J. Zwi Werblowsky, and C. Wirzubski (Jerusalem: Magnes Press, 1967), and presented as a *festschrift* to Gershom Scholem—the other. Strauss had also dealt with this issue in the opening pages of his *Persecution and the Art of Writing* (Glencoe, Ill.: Free Press, 1952). Further comment on the topic is spread throughout the pages of many of the other references in this list.

For my own readings in *The Guide for the Perplexed*, I have used the translation of Shlomo Pines (Chicago: University of Chicago Press, 1963), which includes an illuminating introduction by Strauss, titled "How to Begin to Study *The Guide of the Perplexed*." However, the passages from the *Guide* that I have chosen to quote are in almost every case taken from other translations, which, in each instance, seemed better suited to the narrative flow of this book. As for the *Mishneh Torah*, I have relied most heavily on the translation provided in the Yale Judaica Series, published by the Yale University Press in a series beginning in 1949 and continuing until the present time. I found the translation of the Eight Chapters on ethics from the *Commentary on the Mishnah* in a small volume edited by Joseph Gorfinkle (New York: Columbia University Press, 1912). This appears to have been reissued in 1966 (New York: AMS Press), but I have not seen this edition.

To those familiar with current Maimonidean studies, it is hardly necessary to mention the name of Joel Kraemer. Whether as essayist, commentator, editor, or book-length author, he has made numerous contributions, and each of his works is well worth reading. Most recent is his essay "Moses Maimonides, an Intellectual Portrait," in *The Cambridge Companion to Maimonides* (Cambridge: Cambridge University Press, 2005).

The material on Maimonides as physician is derived from multiple sources, including those that describe the state of medical knowledge as it existed in medieval Europe and the Muslim lands. For this period and its precedents, I have returned to my own *Doctors: The Biography of Medicine* (New York: Knopf, 1988), including not only its text but certain of the references in the book's bibliography. Further details of medieval medicine are best sought in a standard encyclopedic text, such as Arturo Castiglioni's classic *A History of Medicine* (New York: Knopf, 1947), or the more recent *The Greatest Benefit to Mankind: A Medical History of Humanity*, by Roy Porter (New York: W. W. Norton, 1997).

Fred Rosner has devoted much of his hugely productive career to studying the medical works of Maimonides and presenting them to physicians and the general reader. He has given us many volumes, which include translations of the relevant texts and his own commentaries on them. Any of his writings are worth looking into, but if asked to recommend a single one, I would choose his collection of essays titled *The Medical Legacy of Moses Maimonides* (New York: Ktav, 1998). Of course, many excellent English translations of each of the ten Maimonidean medical texts are in existence, and I have consulted enough of them to suggest that it is not necessary to look further than those produced by Rosner. Though neither better nor worse than the best of their predecessors, his are more easily available.

The first chapter of the present book is devoted to a discussion of the reasons for which so many Jews, from the classical period onward, have chosen medicine as a career. The texts from which I have sought the answers to this question are many, and I will here enumerate those in which the reader is most likely to derive sufficient benefit to justify delving more deeply. A few of them are perfectly wonderful studies of a particular aspect of the problem, worth reading on their own merits, and the source of deep insight into various aspects of my pursuit of the theme. David Ruderman's *Jewish Thought and Scientific Discovery in Early Modern Europe* (New Haven: Yale University Press, 1995) explores the effect of the sciences on Jewish culture from the late sixteenth to the late eighteenth centuries, embracing the period known to historians as the age of the scientific revolution. Ruderman's book describes the relationship of Jews to medicine during that era, including the influence of Maimonidean thought on some of the prominent Jewish physicians. A book of similar scholarly value is John M. Ephron's *Medicine and the German Jews: A History* (New Haven: Yale University Press, 2001). Another scholarly work is the collection of essays published under the title *Jews and Medicine: Religion, Culture, Science* (Philadelphia: Jewish Publication Society, 1995). Its editor, Natalia Berger, has assembled an all-star cast of medical and cultural historians, including such eminent authorities as Peter Gay, Samuel Kottek, and Shifra Shvarts, to discuss areas as diverse as medicine's relationship to Jewish law, its connection to Jewish ethics, and the history of Jewish women in medicine.

A panoramic and largely biographical approach to Jewish medical contributions is to be found in *Jews and Medicine: An Epic Saga*, by Frank Heynick (New York: Ktav, 2002). *The Jewish Doctor: A Narrative History* (Northvale, N.J.: Jason Aronson, 1996) is one in a series of Michael Nevins's small and extremely enjoyable books on the topic. And then there is Fred Rosner's translation of the classic 1911 study by Julius Preuss, *Biblisch-Talmudische Medizin* (New York: Hebrew Publishing Company, 1978). Another treatise that has become almost equally a classic, at least in America, is Harry Friedenwald's *The Jews and Medicine* (Baltimore: Johns Hopkins University Press, 1944).

Needless to say, a wealth of material on all of the themes addressed in this book exists not only in other volumes, but also in a plethora of monographs and journal articles whose perusal would take a lifetime, as I have found by trying to make a dent in its massive totality. And there are plenty of other books, a good number of which I have read, at least in part. But the foregoing are the texts upon which I have relied most heavily in writing my book. It might be objected that they are not all among the most recent or that several of the volumes of greatest consequence to experts are not included. Be that as it may. I can assure any reader that the works in this listing have been those that have been the ablest guides to this twenty-first-century seeker, looking for the Rambam.